Country Money
国家货币

（英）威廉·怀特海德
费利西娅·劳格里·贝利 ◎ 著
（英）马克·比奇 ◎ 插图
傅瑞蓉 ◎ 译

目录 Contents

4~5　一个国家的经济
我们谁都需要钱。一个国家要维持正常运转，需要的钱的数额非常大。

6~9　国家需要现金
国家的钱都花在了哪些地方？要花多少钱？

10~15　政府如何筹集资金
国家的钱来自何方？谁来缴税？税收的种类有哪些？

16~19　国家的现金
不同国家的货币形式各不相同。你的国家的货币是什么样子的？

20~27　经济
经济指的是什么？它是怎么运行的？

28~29　各国之间的差异
每个国家的经济状况都不一样，因为各国的历史和现实条件各不相同，而且各国经济的运行模式也不一样。

30~31　影响因素：地理
国家的地理条件很重要。

32~33　影响因素：气候
气候也很重要，它至少会影响水资源。

34~37　影响因素：自然资源
你的国家的地底下埋藏着什么资源？它们有价值吗？

38~39　**影响因素：邻国和教育**
你的国家与邻国维持着和平关系吗？邻国的年轻人受教育水平高吗？

40~41　**影响因素：人口**
有的国家人口过多，有的国家人口不足，有的国家则刚刚好。

42~43　**影响因素：劳动力**
劳动者的高技能为什么有助于国家繁荣和富强？

44~49　**影响因素：技术、工业和服务**
发达的现代工业和服务业对国家经济的贡献很大。

50~51　**影响因素：农业**
如果一个国家土地肥沃而充足，那么它也可能像其他工业化国家那样富强。

52~53　**进口—出口**
一个国家可以出口自己有优势的产品，同时进口自己不具优势的产品。

54~55　**停止—启动**
经济有繁荣期，也有衰退期。

56~57　**各出一份力**
将来，你将会参加工作（或者在国内，或者在国外），为经济发展贡献自己的力量。

58~59　**讨论**

60~61　**中英文术语对照表**

62~63　**索引**

64　**译后记**

附　英文影印版

一个国家的经济

你肯定知道,在许多情况下,人们都需要用钱。你也肯定看到过你的父母亲花钱时的情形,因为他们经常需要购买食物、要为汽车加油,还要付清来自电力公司或自来水公司的账单。你肯定非常清楚,你的零花钱是如何被你自己花掉的,或者你是如何把它存起来的,又或者你是如何把它用在了其他你需要用钱的地方的。但是你的国家,也就是你所生活的国家,同样也需要钱,而且还需要很多很多的钱!

不同国家需要的钱的数额有多有少

每个国家需要的钱的数额是不一样的,因为有些国家需要的钱的数额多一些,而有些国家需要的钱的数额则少一些。国家越大,它所需要的钱可能就会越多。然而,有些国家虽然幅员辽阔,但是城市和村镇并不多,人口也比较稀少;而有些国家虽然面积不大,只不过是一个弹丸之地,甚至可能只是一片小岛屿,但是却人满为患,拥挤不堪。

一个国家所需要的钱的多少,取决于这个国家为生存和居住于这个国家的人民提供服务时所需要花费的钱的多少。

让国家运转起来

让一个国家运转起来，必须花钱，而且要花在许许多多不同的事情上。人们需要到处走动，所以必须建造公路、铁路和机场，把各个地区都连接起来。工厂里制造出来的或农场里种植出来的物品要运送到其他地方去，因此，港口和河流也是很重要的。

人们需要接受教育，需要上大学。当人们年老或生病时还需要照顾，甚至有些人还需要一些特殊的护理。

保护公民和公民财产的法律需要警察来执行，国家需要法院来给罪犯定罪，国家还需要建造关押罪犯的监狱。

国家还需要军队来保家卫国，甚至还可能派自己国家的军队去别的国家，以帮助其他国家保卫疆土。

国家还需要有人来管理，需要开展各项活动，因此，国家需要为这些人建造办公室、各种会议所需要的办公大楼……

如图所示。

国家需要现金

并不是所有国家的政府都会把钱花在同样的地方。不过,大多数国家基本上都会把钱花在以下这些方面。

社会保障

社会保障是指为那些需要帮助的人、贫穷的人、生病的人、残疾人、老年人以及失业者提供关怀,有时候还要为他们提供居住的房屋。社会保障还可能涉及其他一些人,比如单亲父母、无家可归者和精神病患者。

工业、农业和就业

政府希望有尽可能多的人正常就业。政府可能会提供一些培训资助,或者直接给农民补贴,以帮助他们种植某些农作物。政府还可能会通过减轻税负,或支持新的建设和开发项目的方式,来促进工业的发展。

教育

大多数国家都把教育放在了它们必须做的事情的第一位。教育是一项昂贵的事业,因为要发展教育事业,国家就必须把学校建造好,并且配齐各种材料和设施,同时还需要对老师进行培训并支付工资。

法律和秩序

无论我们出门在外还是在家休息,都喜欢拥有安全感。国家通常会设立警察机关来确保公民的安全,因此,国家需要钱来支付警察的工资,并为他们建造办公室,还需要为他们支付交通费和培训费。

卫生保健

我们所有人都可能会生病，因此我们都可能需要去看医生或住院。许多国家都制定了国家健康计划，拨款给医院和诊所，并为在那儿工作的医生和护士支付工资，有时候还要出钱购买外科医生和专家所使用的高科技设备。在某些情况下，国家甚至还会支付某些药物的费用。

国防

每个国家都需要捍卫自己的疆土，特别是当它的邻国颇具侵略性的时候。这意味着，国家需要提供资金来建立军队，甚至还需要建立空军部队。如果一个国家有海域的话，那它还要建立海军部队。国防开支是一项国家需要支付的最昂贵的费用之一，因为国家必须为此购买现代化的武器和运输工具。

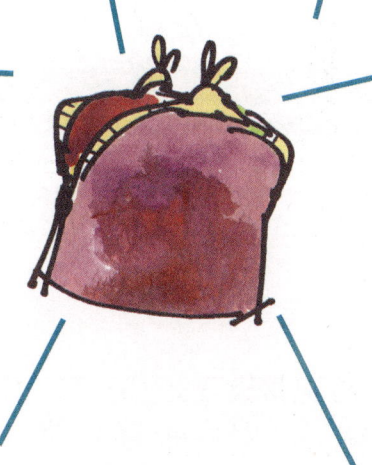

住房

政府需要解决的一个最大的问题是，为不断增加的人口提供足够的住房，同时又要确保不会破坏环境。这意味着要帮助开发商建造低成本的住房，或者建造出租所有权归当地政府机构所有的房子。

交通

对一个国家来说，为了提高工作效率，必须让货物和人员在各地自由流动，这就意味着需要修建公路、铁路和机场。

债务利息

政府所获得的大部分的钱都来自税收，而这些税收是由生活和工作在这个国家的人所缴纳的。不过，这并不总是足以支付所有的支出。当政府入不敷出时，它就必须向银行借钱，同时还要为贷款支付一定的费用或利息。这个还款和利息加起来可能会成为一个国家的沉重的负担。

数以10亿计的钱

当你数钱的时候,你可能是以个位数来计的。当然,如果你数的是你自己存下来的钱,那么或许你可能会以十位数来计;而如果是你生日时收到的一大笔意外之财,那么有可能会以百位数来计。你的父母亲在计算家庭收入和支出时可能会以千来计。但是国家运行所需要的钱,则是以万、百万、亿来计的,甚至偶尔可能会以万亿来计。

10亿是一个什么概念?

把10亿美元钞票摞到一起看起来像什么呢?好吧,如右图所示,这就是10亿美元钞票堆放在一起的情形。而如果把10 000亿美元堆起来,那它就是右图这个钱堆的1 000倍大。

以下是一些有关的数学计算:

100	一百	
1 000	一千	(是一百的十倍大)
1 000 000	一百万	(一百万是一千的一千倍)
1 000 000 000	十亿	(十亿是一千个一百万)
1 000 000 000 000	一万亿	(一万亿是一千个十亿)

10亿

10亿是一个难以理解的数字,但是……

10亿秒前是1959年。

10亿分钟前耶稣还活着。

10亿小时前是在公元前,我们人类的某些祖先还活着。

10亿天前在地球上还没有双脚直立行走的人。

国家预算

国家想要为所有以上这些服务付钱，就需要大量的钱。

例如，在美国，政府会在它认为重要的事情上花费大约 3 800 000 000 亿美元的钱。这笔钱的金额是令人难以置信的。

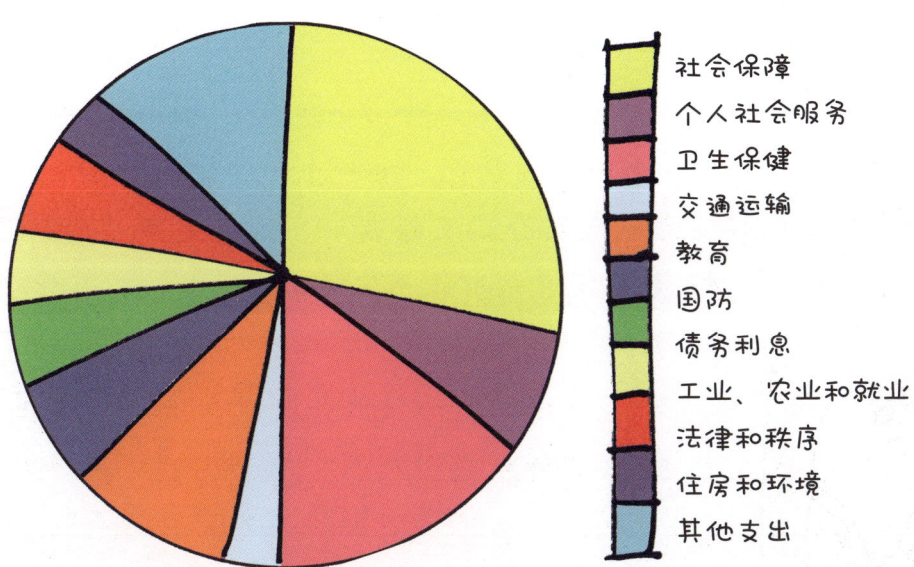

那么，这些钱是从哪里来的呢？

10 000 亿

10 000 亿个便士如果一个接一个地叠起来，将能叠成一座高达 1 400 000 公里的塔，这相当于是人们来回一趟月球后再去一趟月球的距离。

政府如何筹集资金

也许你会认为,只要有需要,政府无论在什么时候都可以随心所欲地印钱。只要开动印钞机,钱就会从里面源源不断地出来。而实际是,对于大多数政府来说,事情并没有那么简单,它们依赖于每个人的贡献。以下就是政府资金的来源……

税收

一个国家的大部分钱都来自这个国家的居民。每一个挣钱的人,不管以何种方式挣钱,都必须把他们收入的一定百分比交给政府。这就是所谓的税收。几乎所有国家都以法律的形式作了规定,凡是有能力获得收入的人都必须缴税。

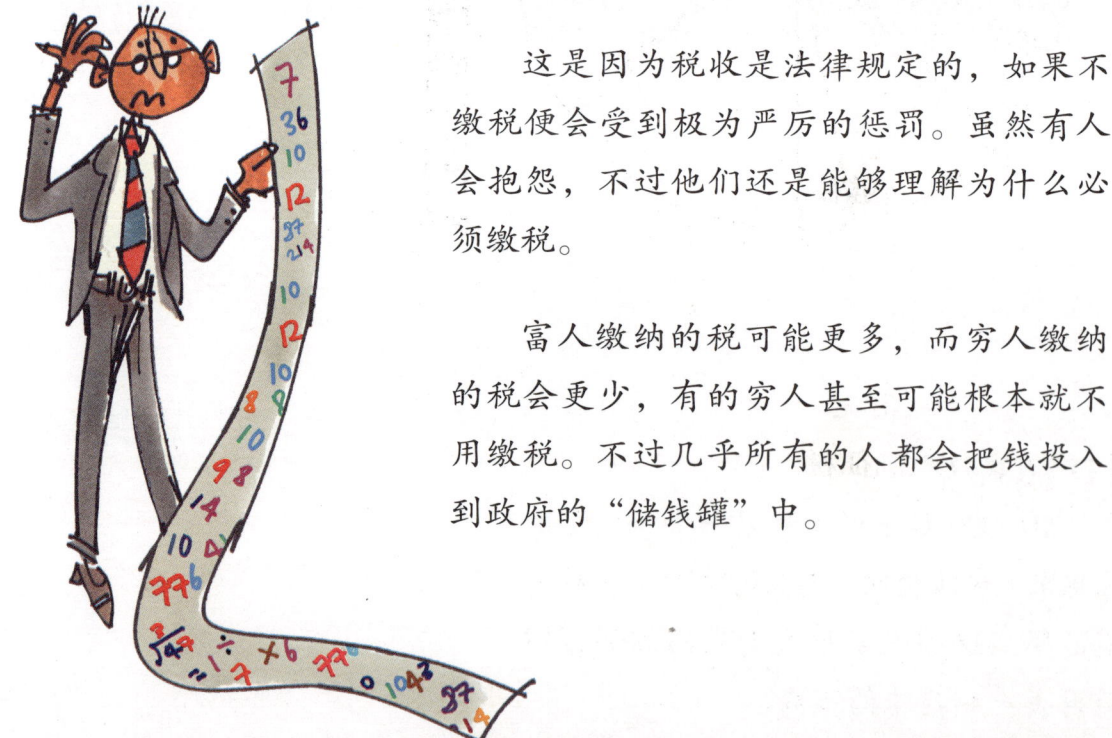

这是因为税收是法律规定的,如果不缴税便会受到极为严厉的惩罚。虽然有人会抱怨,不过他们还是能够理解为什么必须缴税。

富人缴纳的税可能更多,而穷人缴纳的税会更少,有的穷人甚至可能根本就不用缴税。不过几乎所有的人都会把钱投入到政府的"储钱罐"中。

更多的税收

国家收税的途径有很多种。所得税是根据人们的工资或者其他收入而征收的。

但是,税收也可以加入到各种服务中,甚至可以加入到你所购买的商品中。

有一种税被称为"增值税",这种税被政府加进了商品和服务的价格中。这里所说的"商品和服务",是指放在商店中销售的物品,以及产品加工、修理等服务。

有些税能够被加到特殊的食物和饮料中,尤其加入到那些奢侈品和一些对人们健康无关紧要的商品中。

许多政府对汽油和汽车征税,甚至还对飞机征税,目的是减少空气污染。

税收并不是新生事物

印加人是生活在美洲的古老的印第安人,他们居住在南美洲的安第斯山脉地区。在16世纪,西班牙人征服秘鲁期间,印加部落才被发现。印加人不使用钱,但是管理得非常好。

在印加人那里,钱就体现为工作。每个人通过修建道路、耕种田地、挖沟建渠以及修筑庙宇和堡垒而支付他们的"税负"。作为回报,印加部落酋长会支付给劳动者衣服和食物。金和银对印加人而言唾手可得,但是仅仅作陈列之用,而没有被视为钱。

税的高低

税收会因你居住的地方不同而有所不同。大多数国家的政府都试图尽量不向商人和劳动者征收太多的所得税（因为这样才能使政府更受民众欢迎），有些政府甚至根本就不征收任何所得税。

富人多缴税

在大多数国家，你赚的钱越多，你要缴纳的所得税也就越多。一般人都认为，你赚的钱越多，你能为维系国家的正常运转所做的贡献就越大。

政府根据人们不同的收入水平制定了一整套税率，并据此来计算你应该缴纳多少所得税。每个收入达到一定数额的公民，都必须按最低的税率缴纳所得税，比如说收入的25%，还有比25%更高的是40%，甚至还有比这更高的。

穷人少缴税

你赚的钱越少，你所要缴纳的所得税也就越少。在许多国家，如果你的收入没有达到一定的数额，就不用纳税。

政府会设定一个所得税的起征点。每个公民在起征点以下的收入是不用纳税的。通过提高和降低所得税起征点，政府能够缓解社会贫困问题。

富人不用缴税

较高的所得税可能会把富人赶到国外去，他们会搬到那些所得税较低或者根本不用缴纳所得税的国家和地区去。这些地方被称为避税天堂，它们包括卢森堡、摩纳哥的蒙特卡罗和英国的开曼群岛。这些国家和地区的经济依赖于当地政府征收的商品税，例如对汽车征收进口税。在这些国家和地区，国民的教育和医疗甚至没有一项是免费的，而且政府还会经营一些能够创造巨大利润的企业。

每个公民都要缴税

丹麦是世界上所得税最高的国家，最高税率达到68%，基础税率也从42%起征。丹麦的《税收法》是非常复杂的，有所得税、工作税、销售税、奢侈品税，以及企业必须按员工工资的百分比缴纳的各种税。作为回报，丹麦人可以享受免费医疗和免费的高等教育。

税务人员

当然，税收是不会自动到国家的国库里的，所以政府和其他地方当局雇用了一大批人员来管理和征收税款。他们的工作就是确保人们按时足额地缴纳税款。

税务人员的主要工作是监督政府的税收项目，包括对纳税申报和索赔的处理、根据税收目标对个人和企业进行登记、确定会计流程等。税务人员的工作任务是十分艰巨的。

税收有很多规则，因此税务人员必须熟知税法。他们需要评估信息、解释法律、调查纳税申报和索赔问题，然后解决问题。

一场赌博

有时候，一些国家和政府会通过其他方式来向人们筹集资金。在这种情况下，它们所采用的办法更像是某种形式的赌博，尽管这种赌博通常是有益的。

国家彩票

彩票是一种简单的筹集资金的办法，它是通过销售某种预先编好号的"票"来实现的。彩票的销售数量不限，然后在给定的某一天会公布中奖的号码，中奖号码的彩票持有者会赢得一笔资金。余下的彩票销售所得被用来支付教育费用，或者其他一些费用，或者还有可能捐给慈善机构。

有些人不认可彩票，因为他们认为购买彩票是一种赌博行为。但大多数人认为他们买彩票只不过是为了娱乐，而且还能做好事。

许多国家都发行国家彩票。通常销售国家彩票是为了支持许许多多的公益事业，比如慈善事业、体育事业等。在美国，有史以来被赢走的最大金额的彩票出现在 2014 年，3 张中奖彩票的持有人领走了共计 6.56 亿美元的奖金。

政府债券

有些国家的政府还通过民众投资的方式来筹集资金。它会发行储蓄债券，这是一种简单的票据，承诺当你想要兑现时，政府会连本带息地偿还给你。

储蓄债券主要是为了给一些特定的项目融资。

14

印钞票

有些国家极度需要筹集资金，因为它们的经济非常疲软。还有些国家甚至可能会破产，因为它们根本就没有钱。

津巴布韦是目前非洲最贫困的国家之一。14年来，这个国家一直被一个非常糟糕的政府统治着。津巴布韦的工业发展缓慢、农业歉收、出口下降。老百姓每天都在忍饥挨饿，他们每月只能挣得几美分。即使在今天，仍然有95%的津巴布韦人没有工作。

然而，津巴布韦的政府却继续在挥霍，它几乎把所有的钱都用在了自己身上。如果作为一个管理国家的政府，把劳动人民创造的财富全部都据为己有，那么，这个国家的经济必然会受到影响。国家经济不发展，是因为政府收取的钱无法回流社会，企业和人民得不到回报，从而导致大家都不努力工作或者根本就没有工作。

结果，津巴布韦政府只有靠不断地"借贷"或者印钞票，才能继续维持下去，否则就会完全失控。但这样，很快，这个国家的钱就变得毫无价值了。在2006年的时候，你需要3 000津巴布韦元才能换到1美元。过了3年，津巴布韦元已经毫无价值了，最后它被完全废止了，完全不能用它来购买任何东西。

这是津巴布韦发行的面额为万亿元的钞票，但它的价值还不如1美分。事实上，你需要100张这种钞票才能换到5美分

国家的现金

你的国家的货币叫什么？以下所列的是世界上的一些国家或地区的货币，以及它们的特别的名称。

阿富汗的 阿富汗尼
阿尔巴尼亚的 列克
阿尔及利亚的 第纳尔
阿根廷的 比索
澳大利亚的 澳元
阿塞拜疆的 马纳特
孟加拉国的 塔卡
不丹的 努扎姆
巴西的 雷亚尔
保加利亚的 列弗
加拿大的 加拿大元
智利的 比索
中国的 人民币
克罗地亚的 库纳
捷克的 克朗
丹麦的 克朗
匈牙利的 福林
冰岛的 克朗
印度的 卢比
印度尼西亚的 印度尼西亚盾
伊朗的 里亚尔

伊拉克的 第纳尔
日本的 日元
韩国的 韩元
马来西亚的 林吉特
墨西哥的 比索
摩洛哥的 迪拉姆
挪威的 克朗
巴基斯坦的 卢比
菲律宾的 比索
罗马尼亚的 列伊
沙特阿拉伯的 里亚尔
南非的 兰特
瑞典的 克朗
瑞士的 法郎
泰国的 泰铢
土耳其的 里拉
乌克兰的 格里夫纳
英国的 英镑
美国的 美元
越南的 盾

铸造硬币

铸造硬币的工厂叫造币厂。起初，没有人相信硬币具有真正的价值，因此，每个国家的统治者就把他们自己的头像印在硬币上面。

每一枚硬币都出自铸造货币的工厂，这个工厂被称作造币厂。每个国家都会"铸造"它自己国家的硬币。

所有硬币一开始铸造的时候都是一种33厘米宽、457米长的金属条。这个金属条紧接着会被绕成圈，然后送入冲压机。冲压机把它冲压成一种叫做"坯饼"的圆形金属片，再然后把坯饼放入火炉中进行加热、软化。接着再把它放入加热器和干燥机中。这个准备工作还会让它变得闪闪发亮。

下一步就是在它上面刻上图案和字体。这个过程叫做"冲压成模"。把坯饼放在模子上，然后对坯饼进行冲压，坯饼上面就会被冲压出数字、文字和图案。

制造纸币

制造出来的纸币必须不容易被伪造。纸币的实际制造过程有很多秘密。

为安全起见，制造纸币的纸张是用棉纤维制成的。这种纸张还包含有一种不能被影印的特殊的纹线。

图文设计被刻在一种叫做凹版印刷版的钢板上。印刷时这些刻满线条和标记的钢板会被涂满油墨。

每一张纸币上都涂抹有一种特殊的混合油墨。这种油墨具有隐形而秘密的特点。这意味着银行和商店可以使用特殊的光线来检测出伪币。

大多数纸币都有水印设计，它是用模子雕刻到纸上去的。通常，安全线会在水印的条码之间若隐若现。

国与国之间的货币兑换

你肯定知道,用你自己国家的货币能够在本国的任何商店买到任何东西。你会用它去购买你所需要的以及你所想要的一切东西。但是,你可能不知道,货币本身也像任何其他商品一样是可以买卖的,比如说,像糖果和鞋子。有些人的工作就是买卖货币。事实上,全世界每天从早到晚,每时每刻都有人在买卖货币。

外汇兑换

为了购买某个国家的货币你得支付多少钱,这被称为汇率。货币的买卖是在外汇市场上完成的,外汇市场是全世界最大的货币市场。

有朋自远方来

当有国际友人到你的国家来参观访问时,他们是不能用自己国家的货币在你的国家的商店里买东西的。现在,我们不妨假设这些国际友人都来自美国,他们需要在外汇市场买入你的国家的货币。他们在这样做的时候,是根据一定的汇率,然后用美元支付的。

浮动汇率或固定汇率

汇率有可能是浮动的，也可能是固定的。如果是浮动汇率，那么，汇率取决于人们希望或愿意为某一个国家的货币支付多少钱。大多数国家都使用浮动汇率。

固定汇率的意思是，一种货币盯住另外一种比较受欢迎的货币，比如说美元。这种货币的价值会随着美元的价值变化而变化。

汇率

汇率是一国货币同另一国货币进行兑换的比率。是指你购买另外一个国家的货币所支付的钱。

你到底应该支付多少钱，取决于你要购买的货币的价值与你自己国家的货币价值之间的比率。

你必须考虑两种货币，即你自己国家的货币和外国货币。如果你去银行、旅行社或者某个专门从事货币兑换的机构，你通常会看到一张价目单，上面列出了你的国家的货币与许多外国货币进行交换的价格。

两种价格

通常会有两张价目单：一张是关于你购买某种外国货币时所要支付的价格；另外一张是关于你卖出某一外国货币时的价格。

一般来讲，除了在你自己的国家，你在任何一个国家卖出你自己国家的货币都是亏本的。

经 济

"经济"是一个国家所进行的所有活动当中可以喊得最响亮的一个词了。这是因为"经济"这个词，意味着每家商店的每一次微小的买卖，每个人在办公室和工厂里所做的每个小时的工作，每时每刻进出仓库的货物……都进行了加总。实际上，任何地方进行的任何商业活动，都可以称作"经济"。

从家里开始

当你的父母亲早上去上班的时候，他们就已经参与了经济活动。他们一整天都在制造产品或提供服务，而这些就是在为国家的经济做贡献。

你的父母亲得到的报酬，就是你和你的家人所赖以生存的收入。这些家庭收入将用来购买家庭所需要的商品和服务。这种支出就是所谓的消费支出。

通过这种方式，钱会流动到其他行业和服务中去，这样，钱就处于流通状态了。

钱会溜走，又能赚回来，还会变多。

经济繁荣

大部分国家的政府总是努力保持经济的兴旺发达。它们希望看到商业繁荣、货币顺畅地到处流通，也希望人们努力地工作，同时尽情地消费。它们总是希望人们对商品和服务处于高需求状态，同时也希望大家快速地生产商品和提供服务。

为什么呢？繁荣的经济意味着企业会缴纳更多的所得税给政府，也意味着工人会缴纳更多的个人所得税给政府。而所有缴纳的这些税费都将用来为民众提供服务——道路建设、教育支出、医疗服务等。

经济不景气

当需求不足时，经济会呈现出不景气的状态：商品和服务的需求会大量减少，生产也会不足，许多工厂就会倒闭；人们的工作时间会缩短，会有很多人失业。当然，人们同时也会减少消费，从而影响商店的经营状况。

这样，政府的税收收入下降了，它的支出就会越来越少。

我是一个经济学家

很显然，经济学家是研究经济并试图预测将来经济会怎么发展的人。对于那些喜欢整理和归类金融问题并提出他们自己理论的人来说，研究经济就是他们的工作。

经济学家的工作包括许多内容，比如对金融状况的分析、对国际贸易和国内贸易的分析，这些分析涉及自然资源、消费支出、商品和服务的分配、能源成本、银行利率等。

经济学家会建议企业、银行、政府和其他组织采用何种经济政策。如果他们的建议被某个组织采纳，那么，他们就会用数学模型来预测将来要发生的事情。

国内生产总值

放眼世界各地，有些国家经济繁荣并活跃，有些国家则经济萧条和发展缓慢。最富有的经济体是那些与其他国家贸易频繁往来的国家，它们出口如铁和木材等原材料，或者是其他商品，甚至还可能是某些人所拥有的一些特殊技能。

国家经济规模需多大？

一个国家的经济规模是通过计算一年内这个国家所有公民所生产出来的所有产品总价值来衡量的，包括他们所生产的所有商品的价值，以及他们所提供的所有服务的价值。

在计算国内生产总值时，专家们每个小细节都不会放过，都要被计算在内。工厂里生产出来的T恤衫的销售价格、生病的孩子的医疗费等，所有这一切都要被计算在内。对机票和杂货店的支付情况也要进行统计，他们要统计类似的数以百万计的业务。他们要把所有这些数据加总起来算出一个总数值。用这种衡量方法计算出来的数值，就被称为国内生产总值或GDP。

平均收入

平均收入是指国内生产总价值除以这个国家的劳动人口总数所得出的值。这样计算而得的数据表明一个人在一年之内对国家总财富的平均贡献，或者他们在一年内所挣得的国家财富的平均值。

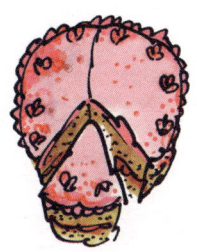

拥有股份

在一个国家内进行生产和销售，几乎肯定是可以增加国内生产总值的。人们会越来越富裕，生意也会越来越红火。

在一个繁荣而又富强的国家里，许多人会通过投资的方式去支持一些公司或企业的发展。他们通过购买一小部分股份的方式把钱借给这些公司或企业，以促进它们的成长和规模的扩大。如果这些公司或企业赚取利润了，那么，它们就会与借钱给它们的所有投资者分享利润。人们通常把这些借钱给它们的人称为股东。

通货膨胀

一段时期之后，所有东西的价格都会上涨。这意味着，20年后的10英镑无法买到像今天这么多的商品。产品成本随着时间的推移会普遍上升。这种情况就是通货膨胀。

各国政府总是努力保持低通货膨胀率，它们不希望价格上涨过快，不希望看到人们在基本的生活必需品上不得不花更多的钱（那样就会导致用于改善生活的钱变得更少）。不断上涨的物品价格往往会使人们的幸福感下降。那些能让人们生活得更幸福的政府会在选举中获胜，而那些没有能力让人们获得幸福生活的政府会落选。

如果一些国家的政府通过法律阻止某些物品价格上涨，或者减少对某些货物征税，或者给人们提供一些钱，用以承担一部分生活费用，那么通货膨胀是能够被控制的。政府提供给人们的这部分钱就被称为补助。

国家经济受到的冲击

看起来似乎很奇怪,但实际国家与你或者你的家人一样,也会出现遭遇金钱损失的情况。在某些年份,一个国家赚的钱没有花出去的多,这种情况就被经济学家们称为预算赤字。这意味着,它无法支付理应支付的所有东西的钱,而如果任其发展下去,时间久了,这个国家就会真正背负债务或者出现财政困难。

经济不景气

经济不景气是指当经济、工业和市场表现状况不佳时的情况。它也指经济活动放缓时的一种状态。例如,当市场不景气时,股票价格会下降,股份投资会减少。

经济衰退

经济衰退是指经济发展速度放缓的持续时间超过数个月之久时的一种状态,它会影响到工业、就业、人们的收入,甚至这种影响会涉及各行各业。

经济衰退一般是由金融机构(如银行)的危险的投资策略所引起的,它既可能损害发达国家的经济,也可能损害发展中国家的经济。

在2008年,美国的投资者投资过度,他们的投资达到了疯狂的地步,最后导致了经济的崩溃。

倒闭了

大萧条

在 1928 年，全世界看起来未来一片光明。美国经济状况良好，投资者们有条不紊地消费并投资着。

许多人试图快速致富。但是到了 1929 年，好日子结束了。在 10 月 24 日那天，股市崩盘了。后来人们把这一天称为"黑色星期四"。到了 11 月，商业投资的价值已经减少了 350 亿美元。许多投资者变得一无所有，紧随其后的便是经济大萧条。

成千上万的人失去了工作，排队报名请求政府的帮助。自此之后，美国花了 10 年的时间才使经济得以恢复，人们才能够再次很容易地找到工作。

失业

从某种意义上说，工作是基本的人类需求。工作让我们感到我们正在为自己有个栖身之所而奋斗，我们正在做贡献，我们是这个社会有用的人才。从某种程度上讲，如果我们没有工作，就会觉得自己是个失败者。

不幸的是，没有一个国家的政府能够保证每个人都会有一份工作。世界上有 22 亿劳动力，但是有工作的人只有 15 亿左右。世界上还有数以亿万计的失业人口，即使在美国和欧洲这样的富裕国家和地区，也仍然有大量的失业人口存在。

谁在管理国家？

一个国家是由许许多多个家庭组成的。有些国家有数以千计的家庭，而有些国家甚至有数以百万计的家庭。一个国家并不仅仅只是某一个国王或王后的国家，也不只是某一个总统或一个政府的国家。在一个国家里，生活着许多家庭，这些家庭的成员或工作，或休闲娱乐，他们饿了吃饭，累了睡觉，他们都会生老病死。他们每个人都为国家的良好运转做着贡献。

谁掌管国家？

当然，如果所有人一起掌管国家，那显然会人满为患的。因此，国家必定需要由某些人来掌管。这些人要确保这个国家的任何一个地方都能够繁荣发展，而不仅仅是某一两个地方。

例如，他们必须确保乡下的孩子跟城里的孩子一样，有地方上学。

我是老板

在某些国家，只有一个统治者，这个统治者拥有很大的权力。有些国家或许是被一个拥有实权的总统所领导，或者由某个富有的家庭所统治。这些统治者决定着民众将如何生活和工作，决定着他们的国家将采用何种经济制度，以及决定由谁来纳税并如何使用这些税收。

选举

在民主国家，人们会选出一群人，让他们代表自己做出决定。被选举出的这一群人拥有权力，其他人都同意遵循他们所制定的规则和法律。这一群人组成的团体被称为政府。只要一当选，这个政府就会行使它的职责。

政府的每个成员都特别重视支持他们的那些选民的需要。这些选民通常居住在全国各地，他们中的有一些人承担了监督国家的职责，比如在教育、道路及卫生服务等领域，监督国家是否很好地履行了职能。

替政府管理钱的人

政府会任命某一个人来管理国家的钱。这个人通常被称为财政部部长。财政部部长是一个非常重要的职位。

财政部部长将决定如何向个人和企业收税，以及收取哪些税，并且还能够决定如何花费这些税款。当然，不同的国家会有所不同。

不同国家之间的税收制度和税款花费有很大不同。

各国之间的差异

国家之间的差异是由什么引起的？是什么原因导致有些国家比其他国家更富裕，有些国家比其他国家人口更拥挤，有些国家比其他国家风光更秀丽，有些国家比其他国家历史更悠久？为什么人们会希望自己生活在某些国家，而不希望自己生活在其他国家？导致国与国之间存在着如此巨大差异的影响因素有哪些？

地理

一个国家如果基本上没有什么地理屏障，比如高山、沙漠、火山和湖泊等，那么，人们就能够轻易地穿行于全国各地，人口便能够在一个国家内自由流动，货物也能够自由地进行交易。

气候

气候指的是某个特定区域的典型的天气。适宜的气候，比如说不太热也不太冷，雨量充沛，那么，这种气候便对这个国家大有助益。因为这样一来，国家就不需要拿出额外的钱来为一些家庭和企业供热或制冷了，而且也有充足的水源让人们种植自己养活自己的粮食。

自然资源

蕴藏于地底下的东西往往是一个国家能够变得富裕的关键因素之一。这些东西包括煤和石油等燃料，铝和金等金属矿物质。这些东西都可以出售给其他国家，从而给自己国家带来货币或其他财富。

政治

谁在管理国家？尤其是谁在掌管国家财政？他们是否把钱用在了刀刃上？他们是否诚实可靠？如果一个国家的领导人是不讲诚信并且贪污腐化的，或者只知道囤积国家资源供自己的亲信挥霍，那么，这个国家的经济就会受到严重损害。

工业

产品都是从工厂里制造出来的。一般情况下，工厂应该尽可能地就地取材，因为本地盛产的原材料更容易获取，价格也更低廉。工厂一般会建造在劳动力资源丰富、交通便利的地方，便利的交通有助于及时运输产品。

教育

接受教育使人变得更有思想、更有想象力。教育能够让人们拥有更多的技能去制造产品、进行发明创造。国家会投入资金让全民接受教育。几乎可以肯定地说，教育投资越多的国家就越繁荣富强。

历史

富裕的现代国家往往都有悠久的贸易历史，它们的国内和国际贸易都很发达，同时还与其他国家友好相处、互惠互利。

工作

人们工作的努力程度往往因国家而异。努力工作的人被称为是有良好职业道德的人。亚洲人民因文化的原因，被广泛认为是世界上最勤劳的人。这些国家的经济也保持着世界上最高的增长速度。

文化

一个国家的文化其实就是一个国家的信仰。每个国家在自由权、财产私有权、投票权和言论自由等方面，都会体现本国的文化和信仰，人们会为了拥有这些权利而努力奋斗。

影响因素：地理

地理因素是指一个国家的地理位置，以及这个国家的地形和地貌。地理位置、地形和地貌对一个国家的富强与否具有很大的影响。人员和物资需要流动，因此海陆空的交通运输都非常重要。高山、峡谷和沙漠会妨碍人员和物资的流通，道路不畅或者港口稀少同样也会阻碍贸易的发展。

海岸线

那些靠近沿海和大洋的国家可以开发港口，有了港口之后，货物就能够被运往世界各地。在16世纪，一些沿海国家，如西班牙、葡萄牙、意大利和英国，通过航运和贸易，后来都发展成了富庶的国家。今天，在美国和亚洲，开发出了许多新的港口，这些港口业务十分繁忙，满载货物的集装箱在港口进进出出。

山脉形成了国与国之间的天然界线

山脉

对于以山脉为国家边界的国家来说，人口的流动以及与邻国的贸易就变得更为困难了。

沙漠

有些国家大部地区都是沙漠。在沙漠上很难种植庄稼，人们时常要挨饿。沙漠也很难穿越。所以，这些国家人口稀少，工业和贸易都不发达。

有些沙漠相当于一个庞大的国家那么大

河流

河流会形成自然边界，因为要过河，就需要修建长长的桥梁，别无他法。

湖泊

有些国家是以湖泊为界的，例如，在美国和加拿大之间，就是以长长的五大湖为自然边界的。

森林

如果森林茂密又荆棘丛生，那么，人们就很难穿越它。柬埔寨就是这样一个森林茂密的国家，它与泰国、老挝和越南都以森林为国界。这些国家正合力制止非法砍伐珍贵的暹罗紫檀树的行为。

边界是障碍

当然，所有这些地理特征都可以被当作天然的边界，从而把国与国之间分隔开来。但是有些边界是人为造就的。这些人造边界的存在是为了让不同国家的人分隔开来，以使他们互相之间免受他国的信仰、语言、文化和政治的影响。这种边界同样也完全阻碍了本国与邻国之间的贸易。

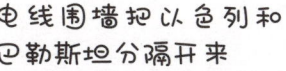

电线围墙把以色列和巴勒斯坦分隔开来

影响因素：气候

气候与天气是不一样的。天气每天都会发生变化，它包括温度、降雨量、风力以及气压等因素。气候是指很长一段时间内的天气的系统表现。

区域

在地球上，不同的地区有不同的气候，每种气候都有自己独特的名字。例如，热带气候存在于赤道附近，那里极少会有极端温度出现，通常都是比较热的，与地球的北部和南部完全不一样。

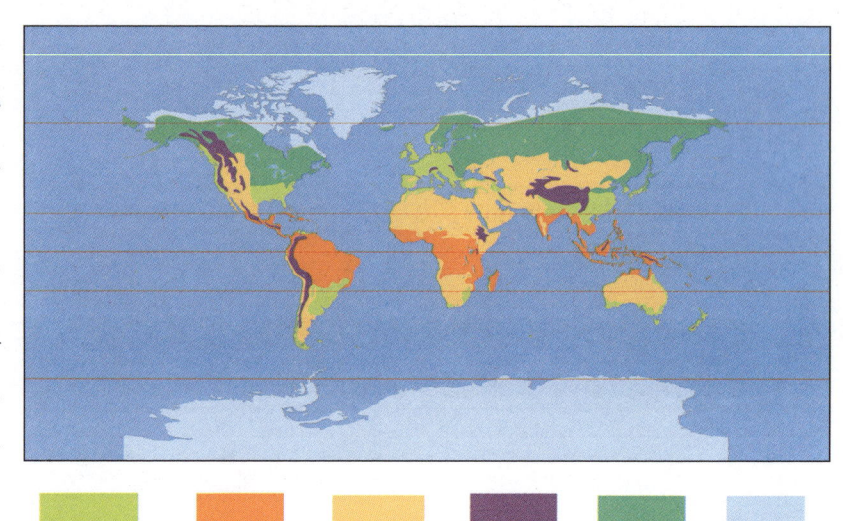

温带　热带　沙漠　山脉　寒带　极地

农业与气候有关

一个国家所处的气候区域会影响到这个国家的经济，尤其是如果这个国家的经济是以农业为基础的时候。农民依靠各个季节的不同天气变化来耕种不同的农作物。

季节性雨季带来的洪水消退后，农民在田里种庄稼

台风和飓风带来的强风、洪水和灾害

干旱杀死农作物,让生命之水枯竭

从空间卫星上观察,飓风在地面上形成了一个漩涡

破坏性天气

如果发生旱灾,农作物就会受到影响。缺水会危害农作物的生长,从而导致农业歉收。这样一来,粮食供应就会减少,农产品价格就会上涨。天气的变化还会导致农作物染上传染病,会形成季风,从而影响收成。最糟糕的,有可能会使农作物颗粒无收。

变化着的气候

今天,许多科学家都承认,我们这个星球的温度正在不断地上升,冰川面积正在缩小,北极冰层正在融化,海平面正在上升,暴风雨比以往更为猛烈,干旱变得更为严重,风暴也更具破坏力。有些科学家说,这是人为因素造成的。我们每天燃烧煤炭和石油——这些也被称为矿物燃料——这些矿物燃料燃烧后所释放出来的气体罩住了整个地球,让地球无法正常地冷却了,从而使整个地球变成了一个温室,产生了"温室效应"。

燃烧矿物燃料就是人为破坏地球大气层

影响因素：自然资源

有一些国家拥有丰富的自然资源，比如石油、天然气、铁矿石、煤炭等，这些自然资源可以从地下开采出来；至于热能和水能，则可以传输到人们需要它们的任何地方，或者也可以就地利用它们作为动力，以驱动机器进行生产。

资源就是力量

那些缺乏自然资源的国家为了求得发展，必须依赖于与其他国家的贸易，它们必须向其他国家购买它们自己所没有的东西。

这可能会引发一些问题，因为愿意销售的物品的价格和数量是由自然资源所有国来决定的。它们可能为了发展本国经济，有意地抬高自然资源产品的价格。不过，这也有可能损害那些对它们国家的自然资源有依赖的国家的经济。

森林提供了建筑所用的木材，但是它被破坏的速度太快了

水对家庭、企业和农业都太重要了

人们为开采金属和矿产而在岩石中钻井

美丽而宁静的乡村是一种自然资源。它既让当地人受益，同时也吸引了世界各地的游客前来度假休息

自然资源很丰富的国家

挪威的石油和天然气都十分丰富，以至于50%的这些资源都可以用于出口。该国大约1/4的国家财富都来自于它，加上挪威人口稀少，只有500万，因此挪威人都很富有。事实上，挪威确实非常富有，连大多数奶牛场的畜舍都装有供暖设备，在寒冷的冬季，奶牛们也不会被冻得瑟瑟发抖。

风力可以被用来创造能量

太阳能可以被转化为电能

自然资源贫乏的国家

希腊是自然资源非常贫乏的国家。这个国家出产的农产品，比如橄榄油、鱼类产品，只够养活它的1 100万人口，由此而导致的一个结果是，希腊必须花很多钱进口各种资源。

一些能源形式是天然的。这是在冰岛从地底下喷涌而出的热蒸汽

影响因素：自然资源——石油

全世界最庞大、最富有的产业是石油产业。石油生产涵盖许多方面，包括石油开采、石油提炼和清洁、管道运输、油轮运输以及对需要它的企业和个人的销售等。

谁需要它？

我们所有人都需要。很可能你在家里就用到了它，也许每天用到它有数百次之多呢！凡是由塑料制成的东西都始于石油。从你的鞋带顶端上的那点东西，到塑料杯和超市里的购物袋，全都始于石油。

石油也可用于制造食品防腐剂、肥皂、泡泡浴液和防腐剂。此外，它还可用于制造化肥、喷漆、胶水和晾衣绳等。当然，如果没有汽油，家庭轿车将寸步难行。

石油为什么会这么贵？

石油是一种不可再生资源。很显然，这意味着，如果我们把它用完了，它将再也不会出现了。这就是它为什么如此宝贵、如此值钱的原因了。

地球为我们提供了丰富的自然资源，我们可以把它们当作能源来使用。在现代，我们用得最多的是矿物燃料——煤、石油（原油）和天然气。

石油源于3~4亿年前生活于水中的植物和微小的动物，后来经过数百万年，这些动植物的遗体被埋藏于沙子和淤泥中，而热量和压力慢慢地把它们变成了石油或原油。因此，我们今天所使用的石油是不可替代的。

成品油被储存于巨大的储油罐中，准备通过海运或管道运输运往世界各地

从地底下抽出来的原油被送往炼油厂清除杂质、碎石和其他物质

汽车是汽油的最大消耗者

汽车是石油消费大户

几千年来，石油都被用作燃料或能源。但是，在20世纪初，由于汽车的大量生产，石油被用于制成汽车燃料汽油。汽油是目前最主要的石油产品。

抽油机

哪些国家抽出的石油最多，以及拥有的可开采的石油储量最大？

* 俄罗斯
* 沙特阿拉伯
* 美国
* 伊朗
* 中国
* 加拿大
* 伊拉克
* 阿拉伯联合酋长国
* 墨西哥
* 科威特

石油资源丰富的国家

在国际市场交易的产品中，石油是最具价值的商品。那么，最赚钱的石油出口国是哪些？

* 卡塔尔
* 科威特
* 阿拉伯联合酋长国
* 土库曼斯坦
* 委内瑞拉
* 沙特阿拉伯
* 加拿大
* 利比亚
* 文莱
* 伊拉克

影响因素：邻国和教育

影响因素：邻国

和平

让一个国家变得贫困的一件事情就是国与国之间的冲突，尤其是战争。战争除了最具破坏性之外，还能阻碍战争国经济的发展。如果一个国家长期处于和平状态，并且与其他国家发展贸易并展开合作，那么，就会有助于这个国家的发展壮大。

盟友

盟友是指朋友。当国与国之间结成同盟的时候，它们与盟友国之间会进行贸易，并且会互相促进经济的发展。盟友国之间通过降低关税，减少贸易障碍，进行互帮互助。

战争是需要花钱的

2000年，世界上最大的灾难之一便是一场战争。当时埃塞俄比亚与它的邻国厄立特里亚发生了战争。数以百万计的美元被花费在雇用士兵和购买军事装备上，这些钱本来是可以用来减轻人民的贫困程度的。据估计，在这场战争中，每天都要花掉100万美元。

携手合作

有时候，许多国家携手合作会让彼此变得更为富裕。它们可以形成一个联合体，使用同一种货币。人们可以很容易地跨越国界，进出口也变得更简单了。

影响因素：教育

在学校里

从你开始上学的那一天起，你的父母就想尽可能地让你接受最好的教育。他们知道，你所受的教育越好，你将来就越有可能得到一份高薪的工作，从而过上更富足的生活。

幼儿园的教育是很重要的

读写能力

读写能力意味着有阅读和书写的能力。世界上所有的国家都设法让它们的人民接受教育，这样，每个人都能增长知识，实现他们的人生目标。在各个发达的工业化国家中，普通民众的读写能力都相当不错，尽管只有挪威才有资格夸耀说，自己国家的国民识字率达到了100%。低识字率会阻碍国家的发展，例如，在阿富汗，只有43%的男性、12.6%的女性具有读写能力，这让母亲们无法帮助和鼓励他们的孩子学习。

许多孩子会花10～12年的时间在学校里学习

大学毕业生正在接受颁发给他们的学位证书

高收入者和低收入者

你赚得越多，你的国家就会变得更美好。那些能够培养出许多高收入者——比如工程师、计算机程序员、医生等——的国家，几乎可以肯定地说，它们将拥有较高的国内生产总值。而在那些大多数人都只接受过小学教育，或者国家财富是建立在小农经济基础上的国家，它们的国内生产总值就可能会低得多。

影响因素：人口

人口总数是指一个国家所有的人的总和。在大多数国家，有关当局要对每一个家庭中出生的孩子和每一个死亡的成员进行登记，因此，人口数字基本上是准确的。

人口增长速度有快有慢

世界人口是指生活于地球上的所有人口的总数。据估计，今天地球上大约有71亿多人口。自14世纪以来，人口数量的增长都一直比较稳定，直到20世纪50~60年代期间，人口增长速度才开始达到最快。但是自从1963年以来，人口增长速度又开始放缓了。然而，人们还是担心，地球将没有足够的水、食物和能源资源来养活这么多的人。

超过10亿……

中国担心自己国家的人口增长速度太快了，因此，在1979年，国家通过了一项法律，禁止育龄夫妇生第二胎。尽管大约有1/3的人并不受这一法律的约束，但是大多数人还是遵守的，否则将面临巨额罚款。今天，中国的生育法律有所放宽，有更多符合条件的人允许生育两个孩子。不过不管怎样，中国人口的出生率下降了，越来越多的妇女对自己的生活有了自主权。

年轻人的世界

世界上大约有超过 1/4 的人口年龄在 15 岁以下。再过 10 年,这些人都将成为了劳动力。但是,到那时候地球上的人是太多还是太少呢?

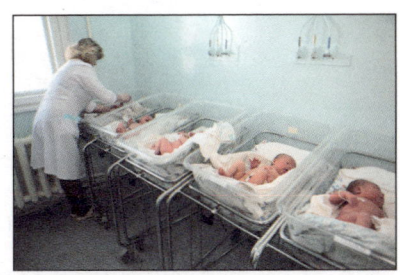
医院病房里的新生婴儿

世界各国的家庭规模都在缩小,这是由于人们的生活水平越来越高了,妇女的工作机会越来越多。但是,在日本,这被认为是一个真正的问题。据日本的新闻媒体报道,已经是连续第三年了,日本的人口出生率都很低,出生人口无法补足死亡的人口。现在。老年人已经远远多于年轻人。在不久的将来,劳动力以及消费者都会变得不够,从而阻碍经济的发展。

有大量年轻人口是一个国家经济健康的标志

人口最多的国家

（人口过亿的国家）

*1	中国	1 364 600 000
*2	印度	1 244 430 000
*3	美国	318 087 000
*4	印度尼西亚	247 424 598
*5	巴西	202 598 000
*6	巴基斯坦	186 527 000
*7	尼日利亚	173 615 000
*8	孟加拉国	152 518 015
*9	俄罗斯	143 700 000
*10	日本	127 100 000

照料老人的费用来自于年轻劳动力的税收贡献

影响因素：劳动力

在许多国家，经济的发展主要是因为有丰富的劳动力。劳动力是指在那些国家生活和工作的人，他们通过自己掌握的技能以及所做的工作来赚钱。

劳动力

在许多国家，人们中学或大学一毕业，或者经过了某种形式的培训，就开始参加工作，直到退休为止。他们大概要工作40年或者更长的时间，之后，他们就可以安享晚年了。

一旦接受过教育和培训之后，工人们就会根据他们所掌握的技能从事各种不同的工作。如果企业经营成功，甚至不断地成长壮大，那么，它就会雇用更多的工人。工人们会用他们赚到的钱去购买各种东西，这样，钱就会通过商店、办事机构和工厂流通起来，从而使得整个经济处于活跃状态。

一个人可能要花费好几年的时间才能完成全程培训，为社会做贡献。

职业道德

有些国家因工人的勤劳而著称。有些工人既愿意为他们自己同时也为他们国家的利益而努力工作。对此，我们说，他们的职业道德感很强。如果一个国家的工人都拥有如此良好的职业道德素养，那么，这个国家的经济就将会得到快速的增长。

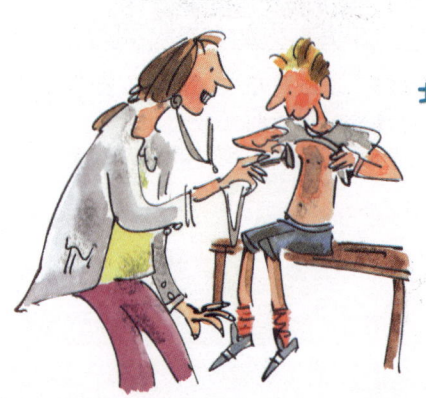

培训

仅仅接受学校教育是不够的，几乎所有的工作都要求人们经过某种形式的培训。

劳动力市场

一个国家可能拥有大量的劳动力（因为总是有很多人是为了谋生而工作的），但是他们却可能没有某些技能，或者住在离工作场所太远的地方，又或者并不乐意做他们现有的工作。

"劳动力市场"指的是工人（愿意工作的人）和雇主（愿意雇用工人的人）走到一起商讨相关事宜的场所。他们将商讨这样一些问题：将要做什么工作，在哪儿工作，工作时间有多长，工资如何结算，有没有另外的补贴，等等。

城市吸引了大量的劳动力，劳动力市场充分发挥了作用

更便宜，速度更快

有些国家可能缺乏一些拥有某些技能的能够完成某些工作的工人。也许这些工作都是单调乏味的，并且这些工作的工资不是很高，因此，雇主们需要从其他国家进口相关的劳动力来帮助他们完成工作。他们或者向国外雇用这些工人，或者可以进口成品。

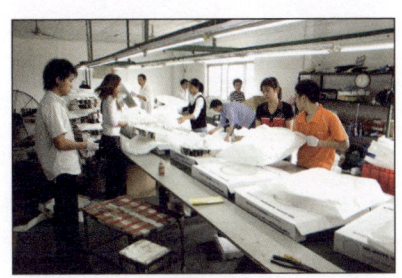

有些工作要求整个团队的成员都有很高的技能

童工

这是一个可悲的事实。在有些国家，有许多年龄不大或根本没有接受过教育的儿童，公司的老板们聘请他们做一些不需要技能然而通常又是很危险的工作，他们的工时很长，但工资却很低。这些人被称为童工。这是一个世界性的问题。全世界有超过1.5亿的、年龄在5~14岁之间的儿童不在学校里上学，而是过早地参加了工作。

年纪小小的工人们（童工）的工作往往是重复性的，他们工作时间很长，但工资却很低

影响因素：技术、工业和服务

影响因素：工业

电脑已经成为一种日常工具，因此人们很容易忘记它其实是一个新生事物。你的祖父母看的电视是一个四四方方的、盒子一样的东西，起初它还是黑白的。如果现在要求你看这种四四方方的黑白电视，你可能会觉得这是一件很荒唐的事。

现代通信技术

众所周知，现代通信技术是近些年才出现的东西。就在几百年前，如果你想告诉别人一些事情，你就必须写信。如果你想知道世界各地发生了什么，你只能通过聊天或阅读报纸得知——如果你有阅读能力的话。但是随着电子科学的发展，一切都开始发生变化了。

现在，在我们生活的这个世界上，出现了许多非常先进的科学技术，大家只要点击或者按下某一个按钮，就可以相互交流和联系。这也改变了人们的工作方式，以及国家赚钱的方式。

技术工人正在组装高科技设备

航空航天技术开辟了新的沟通方式

电脑能够为建筑师设计全息建筑模型图

跟上时代

处于技术革命前沿的那些国家都做得非常好。

这是因为像电脑和移动电话这样的技术，是全世界都需要的。一些亚洲国家在电子产品的生产和制造方面引领了世界潮流。你的手机可能是在自己国家买的，但是它有可能是在中国、韩国和日本制造的。

被淘汰了的国家

没有技术基础的那些国家往往会被淘汰出局。它们不得不进口这些产品，这意味着钱会从自己的国家流出去，流到生产国。在这个时代，我们的沟通方式发生了巨大的变化，这就意味着我们培养劳动技能的方式也必须相应地做出改变。那些提供高科技教育的国家，为科技行业创建了一支非常有用的劳动力大军。那些无法提供高科技教育的国家，则很可能要吃大亏。

创造力

人类的每一项发明都来自于真正有创意的人的大脑。创造力是新的想法得以诞生的源泉。

今天，在我们这个世界上，许许多多公司相互之间都在竞争和角逐，如果某个人有了一个新的处理问题的方法，也就是说，如果他能够跳出"思维的框框"，那么，他就会受到许多创新型公司的青睐。

创造力源于知识。如果你懂得科学、数学、地理学和经济学（又或者你所选择的任何一门学科），而且真的掌握得很好，那你就有可能成为未来的发明家。

影响因素：工业

传送带通过机器按部就班地传送货物

工业通常是指生产或制造商品的行业。在18世纪和19世纪，新的发明创造使人们有可能大批量低成本地生产产品，各种各样的工厂如雨后春笋般地大量涌现出来，那些鼓励这些工业发展的国家变富了。

制造产品

制造产品为人们提供了工作岗位。如果一个国家制造的产品是高质量的，那么通过国内贸易和国际贸易，这个国家就会获得良好的口碑。制造业也有助于货币流通，因为工人们会利用他们的工资去消费各种商品和服务。

基本材料

建立一个生产基地并不是一件很容易的事。大部分产品都是用某种原材料制造出来的。如果所有的原材料都来自同一个国家，那是最好不过的；如果原材料需要从不同的国家进口，那么成本就会上升，这样就会导致成品价格上涨。

"专家"

一个国家如果拥有了合适的原材料以及合适的工人，那么，这个国家便会成为生产某种产品的"专家"。

在美国，汽车产业成了一个专门的行业。福特和通用汽车等公司生产的汽车不仅在美国国内销售，而且也销往国外。现在，日本和韩国已经在国际汽车市场上站稳了脚跟，成功地拥有了自己的一席之地。它们的汽车遍布世界各地。

在英国，一些主要的汽车生产商已经不再参与汽车的生产，取而代之的是一些小型的专业汽车生产商，它们主要生产一些赛车和其他一些小型车辆。

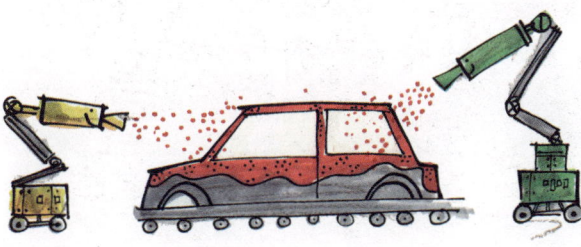

旅游业

有些国家拥有许许多多美丽的乡村、古老的城镇、历史遗迹和一些比较特别的或者奇妙的标志性建筑，它们吸引了大量的国外游客前来旅游参观。人们总是渴望到新的地方去，渴望去看看别人是怎样生活的。

这些来自于国外的参观者被叫做游客，他们需要住酒店，需要食物和使用交通工具，需要付钱买景点门票，需要就地消遣娱乐。他们会把钱花在你的国家。这就是所谓的旅游业。在许多国家，通过旅游业的发展，能获得巨大的财富。

影响因素：服务

与制造和销售产品一样，一个经济体同样也需要为人们提供如银行、保险、医疗和法律服务等业务。像这类服务行业，一般人们的肉眼是不太容易看到它们的产品的，但是它们的产品与制成品一样，也能够为国家赚得很多钱。

发达国家

通常在比较发达的国家，服务业也比较发达，比如在美国、英国和其他欧洲国家，以及一些亚洲国家如新加坡和韩国等，这些国家经济发达、教育水平高，并且劳动力整体素质也高。

一个成长中的行业

在过去一百多年的时间里，全世界的服务业都呈稳步增长的态势。例如在美国，在1929年，国内生产总值的一半都是由它贡献的；50年之后，国内生产总值的2/3是它贡献的；到了1993年，它的贡献占比超过3/4。目前，服务业总计占比超过世界总收入的3/5。

机械化

服务业增长得如此之快的一个原因是，产品制造变得越来越机械化了。许多工作由机器而不是由人来做。产品制造需要的人更少了。更重要的是，可以让更多的人去从事广告业、管理工作和金融服务工作。

办公室工作人员

随着时间的推移，政府机构人员按比例地增大。这意味着政府也需要雇用更多的人。所有这些政府雇员都属于服务行业。

当然，在许多服务行业中还有许多办公室工作人员。

服务行业

全世界排名在前20位的服务业：

* 广告业
* 儿童保健公司
* 娱乐产业
* 金融服务业
* 卫生保健
* 旅游接待业——酒店
* 保险业
* 律师、法律服务业
* 营销和销售行业
* 在线服务业
* 旅游业
* 旅行。

影响因素：农业

农业是一个非常重要的产业，而种植业则是农业的一个组成部分。在人类历史上，种植业曾经是一个最重要的产业，因为它为国家的民众提供食物，并且还可以用多余的粮食换取其他东西。今天，世界上从事农业生产的人数已经很少了，但是农业仍然跟过去一样，是一个重要的产业。

自给自足

通常而言，自给自足型农业的意思是，农民自己生产产品供自己使用。一个自给自足的农场通常种植供农场主自己家庭所需的粮食作物，或只养殖供他自己家庭所需要的动物，很少有或几乎没有剩余的物品拿来交易或出售。

然而，许多自耕农总是试图把自己多余的农产品拿出去交易，以换取他们自己无法生产的产品，如糖、服装和铁屋顶。大多数自给自足的农民生活在非洲和亚洲的一些贫困的或发展中的国家的农村里。有些国家已经开发出了一些贸易项目，利用他们的特殊技能和当地的原材料与其他国家建立贸易联系。

过剩

当农民主要是为了销售而种植农作物时，有时候会出现种得太多，因而农产品无法全部卖出去的情况。这种情况就叫做产品过剩。你可能会认为，处理这些过剩的小麦或奶油的最好的办法是，把它们捐赠给那些贫困国家的饥饿的人民。但是这样做并不合适，因为它通常会降低进口国商品的价格，使种植农作物的农民将没有多大的利润可赚。

那么，将如何处置这些剩余的农产品呢？有时候把它堆放在一起，然后任它腐烂。更有可能是进行"倾销"，也就是说，把它们以非常低的价格卖出去。

大面积种植的油菜，提供了丰富的菜籽油

堆积如山的剩余小麦

补贴

有些国家的政府会不时地通过发放补贴的形式帮助农民。补贴是国家财政补助的一种方式。它可以体现为多种形式：直接给予金钱资助，减税，或者以低价提供某些能源，如水等。

公平贸易

公平贸易是一个政策，以用来帮助一些发展中国家的贫困农民。它的目的是确保这些国家生产出口商品的农民，不会因为不公平的贸易和关税而受到剥削或者亏本。咖啡产业和香蕉产业的公平贸易计划，就是当前贸易的一个例子。

不幸的是，发展中国家贫穷的农民生产出来的产品很难在富裕国家的市场上竞争，富裕国家需要高质量的产品，而对贫穷的农民来说，这是不太可能做到的。

利用人力运输物资

规模不大的捕捞活动已经足够渔民养活全家了

使用传统的耕作方式

摊主在市场上销售剩余的产品

进口一出口

大多数国家往往集中精力生产那些比其他国家更有优势或者生产成本更低的商品和服务。如果他们生产出来的产品供过于求了,那么,他们就把这些多余的产品拿来与其他国家进行交易。

出口

出口是指一个国家提供的商品和服务被别的国家的公司或政府所购买。大量出口或销售货物到国外对一个国家来说是非常有利的,因为它会给这个国家带来现金并创造财富。

进口

商品和服务被运进本国来进行销售,叫做进口。进口需要花掉国家的钱,因为进口商品的公司必须为这些商品付钱,因此,钱是从国内流到国外去的。

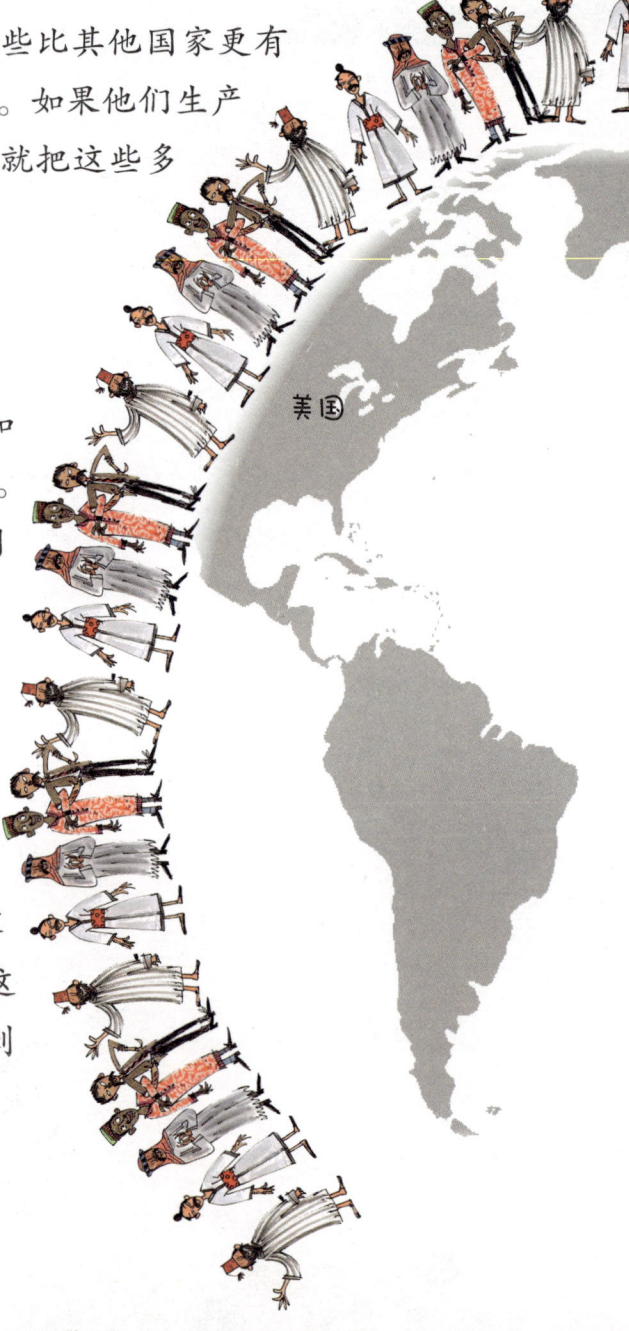

美国

保持进出口平衡

一个国家的贸易平衡与这个国家从国外买进的商品和销售到国外的商品有关。

一个国家销往国外的商品与从国外买进的商品之间的差额就是贸易差额。

但是，大多数国家并不希望从国外买进的商品额与销往国外的商品额之间存在太大的差额。总是设法在进口与出口之间寻找平衡，这种平衡就被称为贸易平衡。因此，当某些国家大量出口商品时，同时也倾向于进口大量商品。

中国

全球最大的出口国

中国的出口超过任何其他国家。

全球最大的进口国

美国的进口超过任何其他国家。

停止—启动

很多人认为政府不应该过多地干预国家经济，他们认为，商人知道他们正在做什么，也知道如何赚钱。

自由贸易

那些支持自由市场经济的人认为，当政府干预过多时，企业便不能够正常地运转了。企业主应该自主决定付多少工资给工人，以及出口多少货物。这就是说，企业主应该拥有自主经营的权利。

他们认为，如果他们不能实现利润最大化，那么，企业主就会失去发展业务的兴趣。

贸易管制

其他一些人认为，政府应该参与到商业活动中去，政府能够帮助企业的发展。

根据这种观点，企业必须遵照并执行政府制定的政策。除此之外，政府可以制定有助于本国贸易发展的规章制度，也可以制定规则阻止其他国家发展这项业务。国家是通过在自由市场上采取干预的措施而实现这一点的。国家设置障碍阻止竞争，这就是通常所说的贸易壁垒。

贸易壁垒

阻碍贸易发展的任何措施都是贸易壁垒。

关税是一种特殊的税收，它通常只对进口商品进行征税，它能够使进口商品的价格变得更昂贵。关税的目的是使国内同类商品比国外进口的商品更便宜。

配额能够在一定时期内限制进口货物的数量。当然，国内企业不会受到这样的限制。

产品标准也可以成为一种贸易壁垒，例如，有些国家不允许进口转基因（GM）的牛肉和小麦。这同样也保护了进口国农民免于竞争。

一个稳定的政府

有些国家的政府经常更替，而另外有些国家的政府则通常有一个固定的任职期限，一般为四年。

假设政府参与到商业活动中去，帮助企业为国家创造财富，而如果政府经常更替，那就不是一件好事情了。更迭后的政府可能会制定一些新的规章制度要求企业执行，而企业可能对旧的规章制度比较适应。因此，一个稳定的政府，也就是一个拥有固定任职期限的政府，这样更有利于企业的发展。

各出一份力

无论你身在何处,你都希望当你成年之后,能为国家经济的发展做出贡献。无论你是一名律师、护士、出租车司机,还是从事其他什么职业,实际上你都能够为创造国家的财富出一份力。

接受教育

要想为国家出力,得先接受教育。大多数发达国家都提供了免费教育,至少从小学到高中阶段。政府提供义务教育,以确保学龄孩子能够获得一些基本技能,比如阅读能力、基本的运算能力以及计算机操作能力,从而将来得以谋生。

高等教育是为那些需要学习更专业的知识的学生准备的。大学学位可以有助于你的未来职业生涯,而技术学院的教育则是为你进入某一具体行业做准备的。

选择一个职业

你可能从小就非常擅长某些方面,这种兴趣会引导你将来从事某种特殊的职业。例如,如果你的数学非常不错,那么,你可能想将来当一名教师;或者你想获得一个物理学学位,从事天文学方面的工作。如果你不知道你想选择哪个职业,那么,你可以寻求学校里就业指导老师的帮助,让他们帮你选择适合自己的职业。

接受培训

离开学校后，你的教育并未结束。在工作中，你要接受专业技能的培训。公司会为你提供实习的机会，让你一边工作一边学习掌握一门技能。其他机构也会提供一些培训课程，以帮助你掌握一些基本技能。

工作地点

许多国家都有一些专门从事特殊工作的地方。例如，在美国的加利福尼亚州，有一个科技人员汇集的地方，被称为硅谷。在英国的伦敦，有一个金融业蓬勃发展的地方，叫做金融城。如果你想从事某种特定的工作，那么，你就得搬到有这些工作聚集的场所去。

今天，人口流动更为频繁，人们更愿意为了工作而选择一个更合适的地方生活。人口的流动促进了经济的发展，虽然有些人会认为，一个地区的繁荣意味着另一个地区的衰败，工作机会应该分布得更均匀一些。

你的贡献

一旦你开始工作了，你就在为国家经济的发展做贡献了。你的贡献体现在你缴纳的税收以及你所花费的钱上。无论是你买了一辆汽车、一套房子，还是一些吃的东西，你都把钱投入到了经济运行中去了，这就等于为其他人给国家的经济繁荣做贡献提供了机会。

再说一遍：不管你做什么工作，赚多少钱，一旦你开始工作了，你就在为国家经济的发展和繁荣做贡献了。

讨 论

税收公平吗？

所有国家都必须筹集资金，因此，大多数国家都会向参加工作的人征税。不同的国家征税的数额不一样。一般来说，你赚的钱越多，你所要缴纳的税也越多。工资高的人比工资低的人要缴纳更多的税，这公平吗？或者说，无论你赚多少，每个人所要缴纳的税额都应该是一样的吗？

印钞票

印钞票就能解决资金问题吗？国家有权力印钞票，它们可以需要多少就印多少，因此，如果一个国家出现财务困难，为什么不干脆多印钞票呢？

通货膨胀是一件坏事吗？

通货膨胀意味着物价的上涨。一些经济学家认为，适度的通货膨胀并不是一件坏事。也有一些人认为，通货膨胀率必须保持在较低的水平上或者为零。为什么对经济发展来说，通货膨胀必定是一件不好的事情呢？

童工的存在是否合理？

在一些国家，孩子们被允许进行长时间的工作（而且只能获得很低的报酬）。这有助于降低商品的成本，增强商品的竞争力，促进经济的发展。但是，使用童工在任何地方都被认为是可以接受的吗？

将来你会从事什么样的工作？

这个世界日新月异，不断地发生着变化，而且以一种前所未有的速度变化着。五十年前的许多工作如今已经不复存在了。教育是怎样帮助你选择适合于未来的工作的？你怎么知道短短的几年之后，这种工作是否还会存在？如果你有大量再培训的机会，是否就能够解决这个问题了？

你设想中的货币是什么样子的？

你能想出一个更好的设计吗？你设想中的货币正面印着的是谁的头像？它是什么颜色的？上面印有什么图案？

你的国家出什么产品？

出口商品和服务有助于一个国家经济的发展。那些能够比其他国家生产出更便宜的商品的国家，它们贸易也更繁荣。但是，这可能意味着低工资和恶劣的工作条件。用这种方法换取出口商品的竞争力的做法是正确的吗？你的国家出口哪些商品和服务呢？

中英文术语对照表

birth rate 出生率
一个国家在一定的时期内，能够衡量和比较的婴儿的出生数量。

brand 品牌
制造商产品的标志或名称，很容易被识别出来。

budget deficit 预算赤字
国家的收入和必须支付的款项之间的差额。

commodity 商品
主要指一些比较重要的产品，如谷物和金属，世界上进行大量买卖的产品。

communications 通信
这是一个通用术语，它是指人们彼此之间运用现代技术传递信息的方法。

consumer spending 消费支出
它是指人们如何花钱以及花多少钱。

debt 债务
借来的钱。

democracy 民主
一种管理国家的机制，民众有选择政府的权利。

economy 经济
一个国家的金融和商业活动的总称。

export 出口
向国外销售商品和服务，为国家赚钱。

fossil fuel 矿物燃料
比如煤炭和石油等燃料，它们被埋在地底下，需要数以百万年的时间才能形成。

free market 自由市场
经济运行的一种方式，企业能够自由运作，政府不加干涉。

government 政府
由民众选举而产生并代表民众管理国家的一群人组成的团体。

Gross Domestic Product 国内生产总值
一个国家的总收入，简称GDP。

health care 卫生保健或医疗保健
是政府实施的一个计划，以确保所有民众都能够享受某些医疗服务。

import 进口
从国外购进商品和服务。

income 收入
盈利的另一个名称。

income tax 所得税
税收的一种，一些国家的政府通常根据人们收入的多少来征税。

inflation 通货膨胀
随着商品和服务成本的上升，货币的价值会下降，而同等数量的货币所能购得的商品数量会减少。

investment 投资
把钱借给个人或公司，以帮助他们发展业务。

labour market 劳动力市场
一个国家有劳动能力的人或者能够运用某种特殊技能的人的集群的总称。

literacy 读写能力
指人们阅读和书写能力达到一定水平。

natural resource 自然资源
在环境中天然可得的某些东西，比如水、石油和森林。劳动力也是一种自然资源。

poverty 贫穷或贫困
指有些人没有足够的钱、无法满足自己基本需求的一种状态。

quota 配额
一个国家政府所设定的进口或出口的限额。

raw material 原材料
指如木材和金属等可以被转化为其他产品的材料。

recession 不景气
是一种经济状态，它始于经济增速的减慢，无法赚得足够的钱。

service 服务
由地方政府出钱承办的一些项目，比如修建学校和博物馆等。

subsidy 补贴
由政府出资帮助企业或服务机构。

surplus 过剩
本国不用、外国也不需要的那些额外的物品。

tariff 关税
是国家的政府机构所设置的一种税种，它会使进口商品更加昂贵。

tax 税收
收入或支付的一部分，由政府征收，并用于一些公用事务。

tax haven 避税天堂
税率非常低甚至不征税的国家。

wage 工资
因工作而得到的固定收入。

work ethic 职业道德
为谋生而努力工作的愿望。

workforce 劳动力
在一个国家或一个企业内工作的人。

索 引

The Great Depression 大萧条 25
agriculture 农业 3, 6, 9, 15, 32, 35, 50
bank 银行 17, 21
banknotes 钞票 8
bankrupt 破产 15
birth rate 出生率 40, 41
blank 空白 17
border 边境 5, 7, 30, 31, 34
budget deficit 预算赤字 24
business 企业，商业 12, 13, 15, 20, 21, 23, 27, 28, 34, 36, 42, 48, 54, 55
cars 汽车 11, 13, 37, 47
China 中国 40, 53
climate 气候 2, 28, 32
commodity 商品 22, 37, 50
communications 通信 44
conflict 冲突 38
consumer 消费者 41
consumer spending 消费支出 20, 21
corruption 贪污 29
creativity 创造力 45
crop 谷物 33
currency 货币 2, 16, 17, 18, 19, 38, 59
debt 债务 7, 24, 35, 60
defence 防御 7
democracy 民主 27
Denmark 丹麦 13
distribution 分布 21, 49

dollar 美元 16
drought 干旱 33
economist 经济学家 21
economy 经济 3, 15, 22, 24, 29, 38, 42
education 教育 3, 6, 9, 29, 39
electronics 电子，电气 45
employment 就业 6, 9, 24, 43, 49
energy 能源 21, 35, 36, 37, 40
expenditure 支出 8, 9
export 出口 35, 47, 51, 52, 53, 54, 59
factory 工厂 5, 20, 23, 42
Fair Trade 公平贸易 51
finance minister 财政部部长 27
food 食物 4, 11, 33, 36, 40, 47, 50, 57
fossil fuel 矿物燃料 36
free market 自由市场 54
geography 地理 30
goods 货物 52
government 政府 5, 7, 9, 10, 11, 12, 13, 14, 15, 21, 23, 25, 26, 27, 49, 54, 55, 60
grant 补贴 6
Greece 希腊 35
greenhouse effect 温室效应 33
Gross Domestic Product (GDP) 国内生产总值 2, 22, 23, 35, 39, 48
health care 卫生保健 13, 60
housing 住房 7, 9
import 进口 3, 13, 43, 45, 53, 55

Incas 印加人 11
income 收入 8, 12, 13, 21, 24, 60
income tax 所得税 11
industry 工业 3, 6, 24, 46, 48
inflation 通货膨胀 23
intaglio 凹版 17
interest 利息 7, 9, 14, 21, 54
investment 投资 23, 24, 25, 60
job 工作（可数名词，侧重具体职业）13, 15, 21, 25, 27, 39, 42, 43, 49, 57
labour market 劳动力市场 43
literacy 读写能力 39
loan 借贷 7
lottery 彩票 14
machinery 机器，机械 34, 51
manufacture 制造 17, 45, 46, 47, 48, 49
mechanisation 机械化 49
minting 铸币 17
money 钱，货币 52
national health scheme 国家卫生保健计划 7
natural resource 自然资源 21, 28, 34, 35, 36
Norway 挪威 35, 39 62 63
oil 石油 36
physical barriers 物理屏障 28
plastic 塑料 36
politics 政治 29
population 人口 15, 30, 35, 39, 40, 41
power 权力，力量 26, 27, 34, 35
product 产品 20, 21, 22, 29, 46, 48, 60
profit 利润 23, 50, 54
quota 配额 55

raw material 原材料 22, 46, 47
recession 不景气 24
republic 共和国 26
savings bonds 储蓄债券 14
school 学校 5, 26, 39, 42, 43, 56, 57, 60
services 服务 3, 9, 11, 20, 21, 22, 46, 48, 52, 60
shareholder 股东 23
slump 经济衰退 24
social protection 社会保障 6, 9
subsidy 补贴 6, 23, 51
subsistence farming 自给自足的农业 50
surplus 过剩 50, 51
tariff 关税 38, 51
tax 税收 2, 6, 7, 10, 11, 12, 13, 21, 23, 27, 41, 51, 55, 57, 60
tax haven 避税天堂 13
tax threshold 所得税起征点 12
technology 技术 3, 44
tourism 旅游 47
trade 贸易 21, 22, 24, 28, 29, 30, 31, 34, 35, 38, 50, 51, 52, 53, 54, 55, 57, 60
trade balance 贸易平衡 53
trade gap 贸易差额 53
training 培训 42, 57
transport 运输 7, 9
unemployment 失业 6, 25
war 战争 38
wealth 财富 22, 52
work ethic 职业道德 29, 42
workforce 劳动力 3, 12, 41, 42, 43, 45, 48

译后记

近年来，金融素养已成为培养孩子全面发展的一个重要方面。早在20世纪30年代，美国就开始了对中小学生进行与生活密切相关的理财教育。如今，美国中小学理财教育日趋成熟，主要围绕让中小学生正确地"认识钱、花钱、挣钱、借钱、分享钱以及让钱增值"而展开。在英国，随着金融理财教育的需求不断上升，金融监管局将个人理财知识纳入2008年实施的《国民教育教学大纲（修订）》中，要求中小学校必须对毕业生进行良好的金融知识教育。我国周边的国家如孟加拉、斯里兰卡等，也早已开设了此类课程。

中国的孩子也同样对生活中的金融知识充满渴求。2014年春节期间，《新京报》记者调查了北京90名10~13岁的孩子，结果发现，孩子们平均收到了4 867元压岁钱，比前一年上涨了5%，其中收得最多的孩子，压岁钱有2万元，而一半以上的孩子收到的压岁钱在1 000~5 000元之间。孩子们的压岁钱该怎么处理？一部分家长的做法是直接"据为己有"：要么存入自己的银行账户，要么用到家庭的日常开支及急需的事情上。虽然也有些家长孩子的主体意识和理财意识比较强，但多局限于将孩子的压岁钱存入银行、做定投基金和购买保险等方面。其实，多数孩子都渴望由自己来管理这笔数额不少的钱，但苦于没有一定的金融和理财知识，除了交给父母或买点零食、添加一些课辅用品等之外，也不知道怎么办。因此，及时地向他们普及金融知识，让他们学会理财，应该是时候了。

华夏出版社从英国引进的"华夏少儿金融智慧屋——货币系列"丛书（共4册，中英双语）确实是应时应景之作，它涉及四个主题——世界货币、国家货币、家庭理财和个人理财，它们相互补充，构成一个整体，以孩子们喜爱的绘本形式，把晦涩难懂的国际金融、货币、贸易、经济知识转化为生动有趣的语言，用最浅显的语言全面地阐述了"金融的逻辑"，让孩子们在轻松愉悦的阅读过程中全面触摸金融知识。

完成这一系列书，我要特别感谢我的儿子贾岚晴，这套书献给已是小学生的他。我还要感谢我的先生贾拥民，感谢他一直以来对我的支持、鼓励和帮助。感谢我的母亲蒋仁娟、父亲傅美峰对我儿子的悉心照顾，使我得以安心从事翻译工作。我的朋友和同事傅晓燕、鲍玮玮、傅锐飞、傅旭飞、陈贞芳、郑文英等，也给予了我很多支持和帮助，在此一并致以诚挚的谢意！

感谢华夏出版社一直以来对我的信任！

傅瑞蓉

2015年11月于杭州

附 英文影印版

小贴士

小朋友,为了方便中英文对照阅读,我们排版时尽可能使中文和英文页码一一对应,但由于中英文表达习惯不同,有个别页码的尾行可能会出现不对应的情况,这时,你只要往后翻一页就会找到哦。——编者

Contents

4-5   A country's money
Money is something we all need. But a country needs a huge amount of it to keep things working well.

6-9   Countries need cash
What do countries spend their money on? And just how much do they spend?

10-15   Raising the money
Where does a country's money come from? What taxes are and who pays them.

16-19   Country cash
Countries use different kinds of money known as currencies. What does your currency look like?

20-27   The economy
What is the economy and who runs it? There's GDP and GNP - what are they?

28-29   Different
No two countries have the same kind of economy. That's because they are all different or because they do things differently.

30-31   INFLUENCES : Geography
The land in your country makes a difference.

32-33   INFLUENCES : Climate
And so does the climate. After all, it's vital for water supply if nothing else.

34-37   INFLUENCES : Natural resources
What lies below the ground? And is it valuable? If it's a useful metal or fuel, it certainly is!

38-39 **INFLUENCES: Neighbours; Education**
Is yours a peaceful country that gets on with its neighbours? And does it educate its young people to a high level?

40-41 **INFLUENCES: Population**
Countries can be overpopulated or underpopulated. And some have just the right number of inhabitants.

42-43 **INFLUENCES: Labour**
What do the people work at and how useful is their skill in helping the country succeed?

44-49 **INFLUENCES: Technology; Industry; Services**
Countries with industries and services that are modern and efficient will do well in the world.

50-51 **INFLUENCES: Agriculture**
And if you have vast space and country with rich land for farming, you can be just as successful as an industrial nation.

52-53 **Import – Export**
Countries who make more goods than they need can sell them to others. But goods they don't make, they must buy or import.

54-55 **Stop-start!**
The ups and downs of economies.

56-57 **A part to play**
Soon you will join the workforce of your country – or some other country perhaps – and be a part of an economy.

58-59 **Let's discuss**

60-61 **Glossary**

62-63 **Index**

A country's money

You almost certainly know quite a lot about needing money. You see it being spent by your parents when they need to buy food or petrol, or even pay bills to the electricity or water companies. And you know exactly how your allowance is spent – or saved – or whatever you need to do with it. But your country – the one you live in – needs money too. And it needs quite a lot!

Large or small

Every country needs a different amount because it may be large or small. The larger the country, the more it probably needs. But then it may be a large country but not have so many cities and towns and people living in it. Equally, it may be small, even an island country, but be crowded with folk.

The money a country needs is all about how much money it takes to make things 'work' for the people who live there.

Making things work

To make things 'work' in a country, money must be spent on lots of different things. People need to be able to move about, so roads and railways and airports must be built to link them all together. Goods made in factories or on farms need to be moved, so ports and rivers are also important.

People need to be educated in schools and colleges, and looked after when they are old or sick or needing special care.

Laws are made to protect people and their property. Policemen are needed for control, then courts of law to judge crimes, and prisons where those found guilty will be punished.

And perhaps the country needs an army to protect its borders - or even to help another country do the same.

Then it needs people to manage and help run each activity, and offices where they can work, and a large government building where meetings can take place ...

... the list goes on.

Countries need cash

Not all governments spend their money in the same way but these are some of the things they spend it on.

Social protection

Social protection means providing care – and sometimes homes – for those who need help, the poor, sick, disabled, old and unemployed. This may also include other people such as single parents, the homeless or those with mental illness.

Education

Most countries put education at the top of their 'must have' list. Educating everyone is a costly business. Schools must be built with all the materials and equipment needed. Teachers must be trained and paid.

Industry, agriculture, employment

Governments like to see as many people employed as possible. They may give money as grants for training or subsidies to help farmers grow certain crops. They may help industry by reducing taxes or supporting new building and development.

Law and order

We all like to feel safe when we're out and about. Countries usually set up a police force to make sure you're as safe as it's possible to be. Money is needed to pay for the police, their offices, transport and training.

Health care

We all get sick sometimes, and may need to visit a doctor or hospital. In many countries, a national health scheme pays for hospitals, clinics and the nurses and doctors that work in them, as well as the high-tech equipment that surgeons and specialists use. In some cases the cost of drugs is covered too.

Defence

Each country defends its borders, particularly if it has a neighbour who is aggressive. This means funding an army, maybe an air force too, and a navy if there is a sea border. Defence can be one of the most expensive things a government must pay for, as it has to buy modern weapons and transport vehicles.

Housing

One of the biggest problems a government faces is to provide enough housing for growing populations while making sure the environment is not damaged. This may mean helping builders to create low cost homes, or to build or rent housing owned by local government authorities.

Transport

In order for a country to work efficiently, goods and people must be able to travel from place to place. This means building roads, rail links and airports.

Debt interest

Governments get most of their money from taxes paid by the people who live and work in the country. But this isn't always enough to pay for everything. They have to borrow money from banks and pay a fee, or interest, on the loan, or debt. The repayments and the interest together can add up to a hefty sum.

Billions!

When you count your money, you're probably counting in ones, maybe in tens if you've been saving – and even in hundreds if you've had a birthday windfall! Your parents count the family income and expenditure in thousands. But your country operates in hundreds of thousands, in millions, billions and even occasionally in TRILLIONS!

A billion

What does a billion banknotes look like? Well, the photo on the right shows a pile of 1 billion US dollars, so one trillion would be a thousand times bigger!

Here's the maths:
100   a hundred
1,000   a thousand   (10 times bigger)
1,000,000   a million   (One million is a thousand thousands)
1,000,000,000   a billion   (One billion is a thousand millions)
1,000,000,000,000 a trillion   (One trillion is a thousand billions)

A BILLION
A billion is a difficult number to comprehend. But …
A billion seconds ago it was 1959.
A billion minutes ago Jesus was alive.
A billion hours ago our ancestors were living in 1 BC.
A billion days ago no one walked on Earth on two feet.

Sharing it out

A country that wants to pay for all these services is going to need a great deal of money.

In the USA, for example, the government spends about $3.8 trillion on all the things it considers important. That's an incredible amount of money!

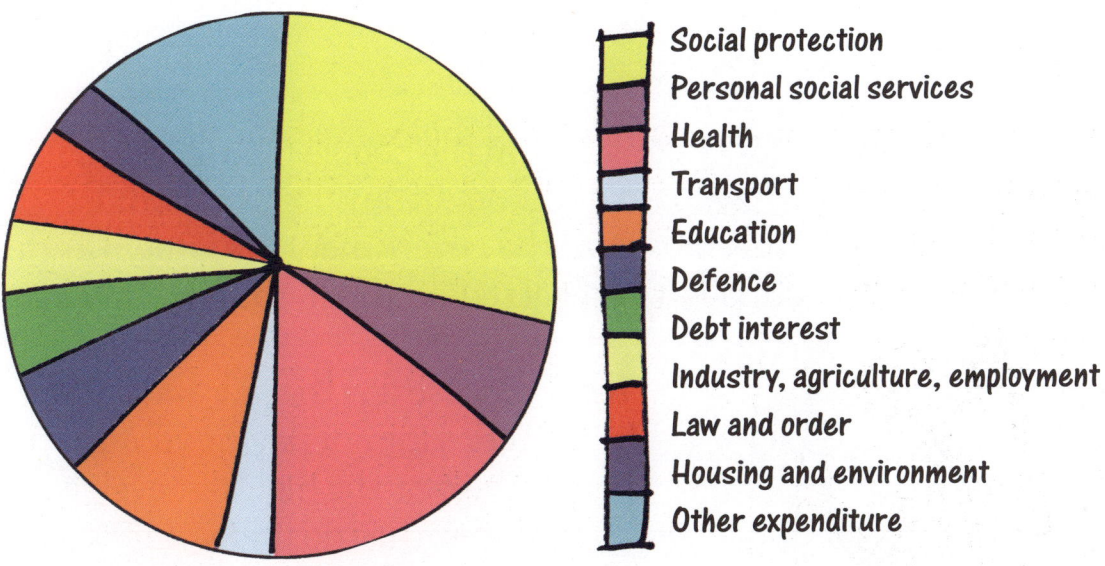

Social protection
Personal social services
Health
Transport
Education
Defence
Debt interest
Industry, agriculture, employment
Law and order
Housing and environment
Other expenditure

A TRILLION
One trillion pennies stacked on top of each other would make a tower about 1,400,000 kilometres high - the same distance as going to the Moon, back to Earth, then to the Moon again.

So where does it come from?

Raising the money

Perhaps you think that a government can just print the money it needs whenever it wants it. It just sets the printing press going and out it comes. Unfortunately for most governments, it isn't nearly this easy. They rely on everyone to help them. And here's how ...

Taxes

Most of a country's money comes from the people who live in it. Each and every person who earns money in any form at all, must give a percentage of this money to the government. It's known as tax, and in almost all countries it's a legal requirement. You HAVE to pay!

This is because it is the law and the penalties for not paying your tax contribution can be high. But even if people groan, they do understand why the payments are necessary.

Wealthy people may pay more tax and poorer people pay less or perhaps nothing at all. But almost everyone puts some money into the government's 'kitty'.

AND MORE TAXES

There are lots of ways to collect taxes. Income tax is collected from people's salaries or other money they earn.

But taxes can be added to all kinds of services too – and even to the goods you buy.

A tax sometimes called 'Purchase' or 'Value Added Tax', is an amount the government adds to the price of goods and services. These are goods sold in shops or bills sent in for repairs or other work.

A tax can be added to special kinds of food or drink, especially those that are luxuries and not considered essential to people's health.

Many governments tax petrol and cars, and even air flights, to try and cut down on air pollution.

Taxation's not new!

The Incas were an ancient American Indian people who lived in the Andes mountains of South America. Inca tribes were only discovered during the Spanish conquest of Peru during the 16th century. The Incas managed very nicely without money.

Money, as such, only existed in the form of work. Each person paid 'taxes' by working on the roads, fields, irrigation canals, temples and fortresses. In return, Inca rulers paid their labourers in clothing and food. Silver and gold were readily available, but only used for display – not money.

High-low tax

Tax is something that can vary according to where you live. Although most governments try to stay popular by not taking too much tax from businesses and the workforce, there are governments who take no tax at all!

The Rich Pay Most

In most countries, the more you earn, the more tax you pay. It's generally believed that the more you earn, the more you're able to contribute to the country's upkeep.

Governments work out how much you have to pay by creating a system of rates for different amounts of income. Everyone who's earning a certain amount, pays the lowest rate – say, 25% of their earnings. After that, a higher rate is paid – perhaps 40% of earnings. And sometimes there is a higher rate still.

The Poor Pay Least

The less you earn, the less tax you pay. And in many countries you don't begin to pay tax until you earn a certain amount.

A government may set what is known as a tax threshold. Everyone can earn this amount without having to pay tax. Governments can raise or lower the tax threshold to try and ease poverty.

The Rich Pay Zero!

High levels of tax may drive the rich out of a country. They move to a country where tax is lower or where tax hardly exists at all. These places are called **tax havens**. They include Luxembourg, Monte Carlo and the Cayman Islands. Their economies survive as the government raises money from taxes on goods, such as import taxes on cars. They may also charge people the whole cost of their education or health care. And some own businesses in the country that make big profits.

Everyone Pays!

Denmark is the country with the highest income tax. The top rate of tax is 68%, with the basic rate starting at 42%. The tax code in Denmark is very complicated, with income taxes, work taxes, sales taxes, taxes on 'luxury items', and various taxes that businesses must pay as a percentage of their salaries. In return for these high taxes, the Danes receive free health care and free higher education.

TAX COLLECTORS

Of course, tax doesn't collect itself, so there's a whole army of people employed by governments and other authorities to administer and collect taxes. And it's their job to make sure people pay the right amount of tax.

The main job of a tax officer is to oversee the tax programmes of the government. This involves the processing of tax returns and claims, the registration of people and companies for tax purposes, and the accountancy procedures to be undertaken. So it's a big job.

And there are lots of rules, so tax officers must know about tax law. They need to evaluate information, interpret the law, investigate problems with tax returns and claims, and then solve them.

Taking a gamble

Governments sometimes find other ways of raising money from the people. They use schemes that are more like games, although they often help a good cause too.

National Lotteries

Lotteries are simple ways of raising money by selling numbered tickets. Any amount of tickets can be sold, and on a given day a draw is made. The holder of the drawn ticket wins a prize. The rest of the money is used to help pay for education or some other cost or, perhaps, a charity.

Some people disagree with lotteries because they see them as a form of gambling. But most consider them just a bit of fun to be had in a good cause.

National lotteries are held in many countries. They are generally set up to support a number of good causes – charities, and so on. The largest win recorded in the USA, saw three tickets win $656 million in 2014.

Government bonds

The government may raise money by asking people to invest in it. It may issue savings bonds, which are simply notes that promise to pay you all your money back, with interest, when you want it.

These savings bonds help raise money to finance special projects.

PRINTING MONEY!

There are some countries that need to raise money because their economies are very weak. The country may even be bankrupt – have no money at all!

Zimbabwe is now one of Africa's poorest countries. It has seen 14 years of poor government. Industry slowed, agriculture failed, and while people in the country starved or earned just a few cents a month, exports fell. Even today, 95% of the population do not have a job.

But the government kept on spending. Often on itself! Where a country is run by a government that takes the wealth created by the people for itself, the economy will suffer. It doesn't grow because money isn't poured back into the country, and businesses and people get no rewards and so work less hard or have no jobs at all.

As a result, 'borrowing' in Zimbabwe – or printing money – just went on until it was out of control. Soon the money had no value at all. By 2006, you needed 3,000 Zimbabwean dollars to buy one US dollar. And three years later, the Zimbabwean dollar was worthless and was abolished altogether. It had no value and couldn't be used to buy anything!

This trillion dollar note was issued in Zimbabwe. It had less value than a US cent. In fact, you needed 100 of these to get US$5.

Country cash

What's your currency called? Here are just some of the world's currencies with their special names.

Afghan afghani
Albanian lek
Algerian dinar
Argentine peso
Australian dollar
Azerbaijani manat
Bangladeshi taka
Bhutanese ngultrum
Brazilian real
Bulgarian lev
Canadian dollar
Chilean peso
Chinese yuan renminbi
Croatian kuna
Czech koruna
Danish krone
Hungarian forint
Icelandic króna
Indian rupee
Indonesian rupiah
Iranian rial

Iraqi dinar
Japanese yen
South Korean won
Malaysian ringgit
Mexican peso
Moroccan dirham
Norwegian kroner
Pakistani rupee
Philippine peso
Romanian leu
Saudi riyal
South African rand
Swedish krona
Swiss franc
Thai baht
Turkish lira
Ukrainian hryvnia
British pound
United States dollar
Vietnamese dong

MAKING COINS

The manufacture of coins is called minting. At first, no one trusted that the value of a coin was genuine, so the rulers in each country allowed their head to be stamped on them.

Every coin comes from a currency-making factory called a mint. Each country 'mints' its own coins.

All coins begin as a metal strip 33cm wide and 457m long. The strips are wound into coils, then fed into a blanking press. This punches out round discs of metal called blanks. The blanks are heated and softened in a furnace. Then they pass through a heater and dryer. This preparation also makes them shiny.

The next stage is to add the design and lettering. This process is called striking. The blanks are passed through a press that strikes, or presses, the amount, words and pictures onto them.

MAKING NOTES

Banknotes have to be made so people can't forge them easily. There's a lot of secrecy about how they're actually produced.

For security, notes are printed on paper that's made from cotton fibres. The paper also contains a special kind of thread that can't be photocopied.

The artist's design is engraved onto a steel plate, called an intaglio plate. When ink is applied to a plate, it fills in the lines and marks.

Specially mixed inks are used to apply invisible, secret features onto each banknote. This means that banks and shops can use special lights to detect forgeries.

Most notes have a watermark design that is moulded into the paper. Often, the security thread appears and disappears between the bars of the watermark.

Country to country

You probably know what your own currency will buy in the local store. You use it to buy goods that you need or want. But money can be bought and sold for itself – just as any other kind of goods – like sugar or shoes. There are people whose job it is to buy and sell your country's currency. Indeed, all day long, people all over the planet are buying and selling each other's currencies.

foreign exchange

How much you pay for a country's currency is called the exchange rate. Currencies are bought and sold on the foreign exchange market, which is the biggest money market in the world.

Coming to stay

When someone comes to visit your country from abroad, they can't use their own currency to buy things in your shops. Let's say they come from the United States. They'll need to use the foreign exchange market to buy your currency. And they'll pay for it using US dollars at a certain exchange rate.

EXCHANGE RATE

The exchange rate is the rate at which one currency can be exchanged for another. It's how much you pay to buy some of another nation's currency.

How much you pay depends on the value of the currency you are buying compared to the value of your own.

You have to take into account two currencies, your currency and the foreign currency. If you go to a bank, a travel agent or a specialist exchange bureau, you can usually see a list of the prices charged in your currency for a number of foreign currencies.

Two prices

Normally there are two prices listed. One price is how much you have to pay if you're buying a certain currency, while the second is how much you'll receive if you're selling instead.

Usually you lose out if you're selling a currency anywhere but in its home country.

floating or fixed

Exchange rates can be floating or fixed. With floating rates the rate depends upon how much people want and are willing to pay for a certain currency. Most countries use a floating exchange rate.

A fixed rate means that a currency is fixed to another popular currency such as the US dollar. It goes up or down in value when the dollar goes up and down in value.

The economy

The economy is a grand-sounding word for all the activity that goes on in a country. It's a word that sums up every small sale and purchase in every shop, every hour of work done in offices and factories, every movement of goods in and out of a warehouse ... in fact, every piece of business going on anywhere.

it starts at home

When your parents go to work in the morning, they become part of the economy. They will spend their day making the products or producing the services that help the country's businesses to run.

In return, they will receive money for you and your family to live on. The family money will buy products and services that the family needs. This is known as consumer spending.

In this way, the money moves on to other businesses and services. It is kept in circulation.

it moves, it earns and it grows.

A good economy

Governments try hard to keep the economy active. They want the money to move around and keep a lot of businesses and people working hard and spending. They want high demand for goods and services, and need everyone to build products and provide services at a rapid rate.

Why? A bustling economy means that companies are paying taxes to the government on their profits. It means workers are paying taxes on their wages. And all these taxes are supplying services – roads, education, medical services, and so on.

A poor economy

A poor economy happens when demand is not as great. Fewer goods and services are needed and produced. Factories start to make less. Work hours are shortened and people may lose their jobs altogether. They have less money to spend, so shops suffer too.

Tax income falls and the government has less and less to spend.

I AM AN ECONOMIST

It seems obvious, but an economist is someone who studies an economy and tries to predict what will happen. This is a job for people who like sorting financial problems and coming up with their own theories.

The work covers a lot of things, such as the finances associated with natural resources, consumer spending, distribution of goods and services, energy costs, bank interest rates and international as well as national trade.

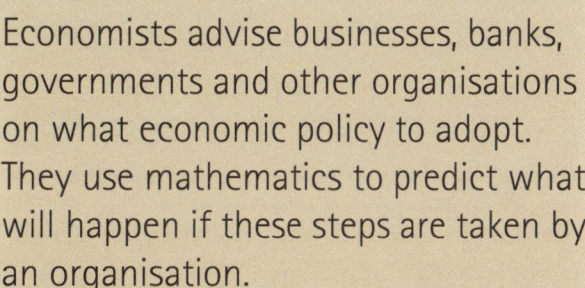

Economists advise businesses, banks, governments and other organisations on what economic policy to adopt. They use mathematics to predict what will happen if these steps are taken by an organisation.

GDP

Around the world, there are countries with bustling, active economies and many that have slower ones. The wealthiest economies are those that trade successfully with other countries. Perhaps they sell raw materials, also known as commodities, such as iron and timber, or they sell other products and even the particular skills of their people.

How big?

The size of a country's economy is measured by adding up the total value of all the work that is done by the citizens of a country in a single year. This includes all the products that are made and all the services that are produced.

Every small detail is known and counted. Economists add up the sales value of T-shirts sewn in a factory or medical payments made to a sick child. They add the sales of airline tickets and grocery payments – millions and millions of transactions like these. Added up, they produce a grand total.

Average earnings

This grand total is then divided by the number of working people living in the country. This produces a figure showing what the average individual has contributed to the country's overall wealth – or has earned – in any year. The measurement is known as the Gross Domestic Product or GDP.

Having a share

A country that is producing and selling is almost certainly growing its GDP. People are getting wealthier and business are becoming more prosperous.

In a prosperous, confident country, many people will support factories and other businesses by investing in them. They lend the companies money to grow and expand by buying a small part, known as a share. If the companies make a profit, they share this with all those investors who lent them money, known as their shareholders.

INFLATION

Over a period of time, the price of just about everything goes up. This means that in twenty years, £10 won't buy nearly as much as it does today. This general increase in the cost of things over time is known as inflation.

Governments try hard to keep inflation low. They don't want prices rising so that people have to spend more and more on basic essentials leaving them less money to live. Rising prices tend to make people unhappy, and governments are chosen and elected because they make people happy – not unhappy!

Inflation can be controlled if the government passes laws to stop price rises, or if it reduces taxes on certain goods, or if it contributes money – known as a subsidy – towards the cost.

Slump-bump!

It may seem odd, but just like you or your family, a country can lose money. If it doesn't earn as much money as it spends, then it experiences what economists call a **budget deficit**. This means it can't pay for all the things it needs to pay for. And if this goes on for too long, a country can get into real debt and difficulty.

Slump

A slump is when an economy, industry or market performs poorly. It also refers to a slowdown in business activity. When the market hits a slump, for instance, share prices and share investment both go down.

Recession

A recession happens when the slowdown in the economy lasts longer than a few months. It affects industry, employment, people's income and all trade.

Recessions can be caused by risky investment strategies used by financial institutions such as banks. It can harm the economies of both the world's developed and developing countries.

In 2008, American investors placed such high values on properties that they became crazily high – and led to a crash.

THE GREAT DEPRESSION

In 1928, the future looked bright. The American economy was in a healthy state and investors were urged to spend and invest.

Many people were trying to get rich quick. Then came 1929 – and the party was over. On October 24th, 'Black Thursday', the share market crashed. By November, the value of business investments had gone down by $35 billion. Many investors lost everything and the Great Depression followed.

Hundreds of thousands of people lost their jobs and queued to sign up for help from the government. It took ten years of suffering before confidence was restored and people could find work easily again.

OUT OF WORK

Working at something which has a purpose is an essential human need. Work is supposed to make us feel that we are contributing, being useful, earning our place on the planet. We are also made to feel that we're somehow failing if we're not working.

Unfortunately, no country can guarantee jobs for everyone. Of the 2.2 billion people in the world's labour force, 1.5 billion or so are employed. There are millions of unemployed people, even in the richer countries of the USA and Europe.

Who runs the country?

A country is made up of lots of families. Thousands, sometimes millions of them. A country is not just a king or queen. It's not just a president or a government. It's lots and lots of people living in family groups who work and play, eat and sleep, live and die. And the country must be run so they can all function.

Who's in charge?

Of course, there are far too many people to all run the country together. So someone has to be in charge! Someone has to make sure that things work in every part of the country and not just in one or two places.

For example, they have to make sure that children who live in the countryside have schools to attend as well as those who live in the cities.

I'm boss!

In some countries, there is a ruler who has a lot of power. Or perhaps it's a president who holds the power. Or a rich family. These people will decide how others live and work. They will decide what kind of economy operates in their country. They will decide who pays taxes and how the taxes are spent.

Elected

In countries known as democracies, the population will choose a group of people who will make the decisions on their behalf. This group is elected to hold power, and everyone else agrees to follow the rules and laws that they lay down. The group is known as the government and they do this work for as long as they are elected.

Each member of a government pays special attention to the needs of the group of people who elected them, those who live in a particular area. Then some of them take on the extra work of supervising the country's education, or roads, or health needs.

The money man

One person in the government is given the job of looking after the country's money. In some countries he is known as the Finance Minister, and in others, the Treasurer. This is a very important post.

The Finance Minister will decide what decisions are taken on the taxes collected from people and businesses, and how they are spent.

And that will vary from country to country.

Different

What makes countries different? What makes one country seem wealthier or more crowded or more beautiful or historic than another? Why do people want to live in some countries and not in others? What are the influences that make countries so different?

Geography

A country with fewer physical barriers, mountains, deserts, volcanoes, lakes and so on, is easier to travel in. People and goods can move more freely to work and trade with each other.

Climate

Climate describes the weather that is typical to a particular region. A moderate climate – not too hot or cold with enough rainfall to keep water supplies flowing – is a great help to a country. Money is not needed for extra heating or cooling of homes or businesses, and water helps grow crops to feed the people.

Natural Resources

What lies hidden below the ground is often a key to how successful a country can become. Fuels such as coal and oil, or metals and minerals such as aluminium or gold, can be sold to other countries and create wealth.

Politics

Who runs the country and especially its finances? Do they spend wisely? Are they honest? A country's economy might suffer through dishonesty of its leaders and the corruption and hoarding of the country's resources.

Industry

Factories make products. They use materials that can be found locally if possible, as these will be easier to get and probably cheaper. Factories are built where there are people to help make them, and roads to move them when finished.

Education

Getting educated is about becoming a person with ideas and imagination. It's about having the skills to make and create. A country that invests in education for all its people, will almost certainly prosper more than one that doesn't.

• •

History

Modern successful countries often have a long history of trade, of travel across continents, and friendship with other countries who they may have helped at one time or another.

Work

How hard people work tends to vary from country to country. Those who work hard are said to have a good **work ethic**. The Asian culture is widely known to be the hardest working. The economies of these countries have the highest growth rate.

Culture

A country's culture is all about what it believes in. Every country has beliefs, such as the right to be free, to own property or vote, or the right to say what you think. People who are proud of these will work hard to keep them.

Influences: Geography

Geography, the position of a country and the kind of land it has, can make a difference to how successful it is. People and goods need to move, so transport by land, sea and air, is helpful. When mountains, canyons or deserts get in the way of this, or there are few roads or sea ports, trade becomes difficult.

Coasts

Countries with a border on a sea or ocean can develop ports from which its goods can be sent around the world. In the 16th century, coastal countries such as Spain, Portugal, Italy and Britain, became wealthy through shipping and trade. Today, new ports in Asia and the USA among others, service loaded container ships carrying all kinds of goods in and out.

Mountains

When a country has a mountainous border, it becomes more difficult to move from place to place and trade with neighbouring countries.

Mountain ranges form a natural barrier between countries.

Deserts

Some countries are made up of mostly desert. Here, it's difficult to grow crops and people can go hungry. Deserts are also difficult to cross, the population is low, and industry and trade are limited.

A desert can be the size of a large country.

Rivers
Rivers form a natural border as they may need long bridges to cross, and cannot be crossed elsewhere.

Lakes
Several countries may border a lake. The string of the five Great Lakes forms a natural border between the USA and Canada, for example.

Forests
Forests can be thick and so tangled that they are impossible to move through. Cambodia is a heavily forested country that shares forest borders with Thailand, Laos and Vietnam. These countries are now working together to stop illegal cutting of valuable Siamese rosewood trees.

• • • • • • • • • • • • • • • • •

Borders as barriers
Of course, all these geographical features can be used as natural borders, separating one country from another. But some borders are man-made. They exist to keep people apart, to protect them from each other's beliefs, language, culture or politics. Such borders also completely block trade between neighbours.

A wire fence separates Israel and Palestine.

31

Influences: Climate

Climate is not the same as weather. Weather is what happens from day to day. It includes the temperature, how much rainfall there will be, the strength of the wind, and other factors as well such as air pressure. Climate is how weather systems behave over a long period of time.

Zones

Different climates exist in different zones of the Earth and they have specific names. Tropical climates, for example, occur around the equator where there are few temperature extremes. Here it is usually hot, unlike areas to the north and south.

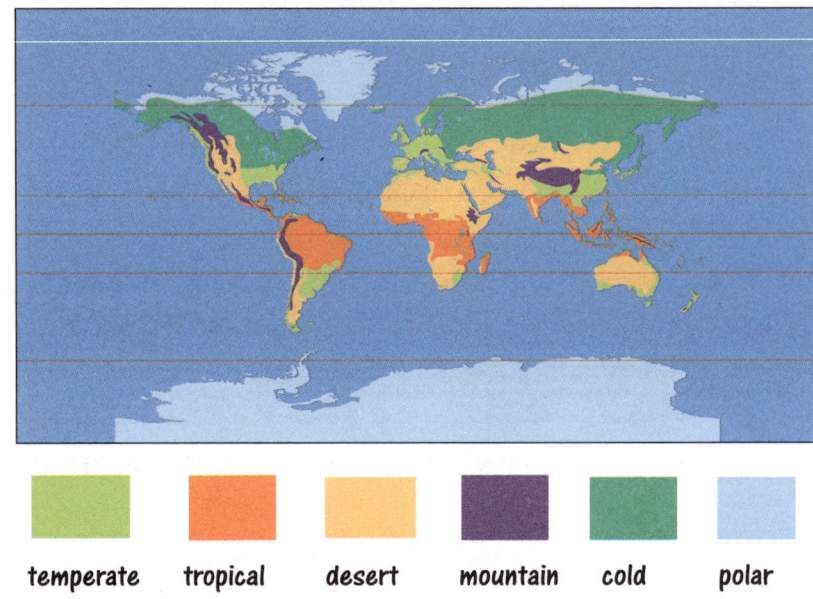

temperate   tropical   desert   mountain   cold   polar

Rice farmers flood their fields for planting after the seasonal monsoon rains.

Planting weather

The climate zone in which a country exists can have an influence on its economy, especially if its economy is based on agriculture. Farmers rely on the seasons to bring certain kinds of weather to help crops grow.

Typhoons and hurricanes bring strong winds, floods and damage.

Droughts kill crops and dry up vital water supplies for people.

A hurricane, viewed from a space satellite, can be seen swirling above the land.

Damaging Weather

If there is a drought, crops will suffer. The lack of water will damage growth so there will be less to harvest. As a result, there will be less food to go around and prices will go up. A change in weather patterns can also encourage infectious diseases in plants, cause monsoons, prevent crops from being harvested, or at worst, destroy an entire crop.

Changing Climate

Today, scientists agree that our planet is warming up. Glaciers are shrinking, the Arctic ice is melting, sea levels are rising, and storms are more violent. Droughts are more severe, and storms are more destructive. Some scientists say that it is humans who have caused this to happen. Every day we burn coal and oil – also known as fossil fuels – and the fumes from this have increased gases which shield the Earth from normal cooling in a "greenhouse" effect.

Burning fossil fuels has contributed to the man-made destruction of Earth's atmosphere.

Influences: Natural resources

Some countries have access to natural resources such as oil, gas, iron ore, or coal within their own borders. They can mine these from the ground, or in the case of heat or water, they can move it where it's needed or use it to power machinery.

Resources are power

However, those countries without natural resources have to rely on trade with countries that do have them in order to develop. They have to buy what they don't have.

This can cause problems because the countries with the natural resources can say how much they will cost and how much they might be willing to sell. They can put up prices in order to help their own economy, but this may damage the economy of other countries that rely on them.

Forests provide timber for building but can be destroyed too fast.

Water is essential for homes, businesses and farming.

Mining and tunnelling through rock for metals and minerals.

Beautiful and peaceful countryside is a natural resource. It benefits the people who live there but can attract overseas visitors on holiday.

The power of the wind can be harnessed to create energy.

And the heat of the sun can be converted to electricity.

Some energy forms are natural. Hot steam pours from underground in Iceland.

i Have

Norway has so much oil and natural gas that it can export 50% of it. This makes up about a quarter of Norway's wealth, and its small population of 5 million people are wealthy. In fact, the country is so wealthy that most of its dairy farms have heated barns so the cows don't shiver during their cold winters!

i Don't Have

Greece, on the other hand, has very few natural resources. It has agricultural goods such as olive oil, and fish. It has just enough to feed its 11 million population. As a result, Greece has to pay out to import other goods and its energy needs, and, as a result, its level of debt is high.

Influences: Natural resources: OIL

The largest and wealthiest industry in the world is oil production. This means everything to do with getting it out of the ground, refining or cleaning it, moving it through pipes or by tanker from place to place, and selling it to businesses and individuals who need it.

Who needs it?

We all do! It's likely you use it in the home – hundreds of times a day! Anything made of plastic started with oil, from the tips on your shoelaces to plastic cups and the bags at the supermarket.

Oil is also in food preservatives, soap, bubble bath and antiseptic cream. Outside, it's in fertilisers, spray paint, glue and the clothes line. And the family car may not move without petrol – or oil.

Why expensive?

Oil is a non-renewable energy source. That means quite simply that when we run out, there's no more left. And that's why it's precious. And valuable!

Earth provides us with plenty of natural resources that can be used as a source of energy. Those we've been using a lot in modern times are fossil fuels – coal, petroleum (crude oil) and natural gas.

Oil started as plants and tiny animals that lived in water 300 to 400 million years ago. Over millions of years, the remains of these animals were covered in sand and silt. Heat and pressure slowly turned them into oil, or petroleum. So the oil we use today cannot possibly be replaced.

Refined oil is stored in huge containers ready to be shipped or piped worldwide

Crude oil, pumped from underground, is brought to the refinery where it is cleaned of impurities, bits of rock and other materials.

Cars are the single largest users of petrol.

Car Guzzlers

Oil has been used as a fuel, or energy source, for thousands of years. But when mass production of cars began at the beginning of the 20th century, oil was turned into petrol to fuel them. Petrol is now the main oil product.

★ Oil Pumpers

Who pumped out the most and has the largest reserves still to pump?
* Russia
* Saudi Arabia
* United States
* Iran
* China
* Canada
* Iraq
* United Arab Emirates
* Mexico
* Kuwait

★ Oil Rich!

Oil is the most valuable commodity traded on world markets. So who made the most money from exporting it?
* Qatar
* Kuwait
* UAE
* Turkmenistan
* Venezuela
* Saudi
* Canada
* Libya
* Brunei
* Iraq

Influences: Neighbours; Education

Influences: Neighbours

Peace
One of the things that stops a country from becoming wealthy is conflict, especially war. Apart from the destruction, wars stop countries from developing. Long periods of peace where countries trade and co-operate with each other, help growth and development.

Allies
Allies means friends. When countries have allies, they can trade with those allies and help the countries involved to grow their economies. Allies help each other by reducing special taxes known as tariffs and making trade easier.

Wars cost money
One of the worst disasters happened in 2000 when the country of Ethiopia was at war with its neighbour Eritrea. Millions of dollars were spent on soldiers and military equipment that could have been used to reduce the people's poverty. It is estimated that $1 million a day was being spent on the war.

Working together
Sometimes countries find it easier to work together to become wealthier. They may form unions that use the same currency. Borders are easier to cross, which makes importing and exporting easier.

Influences: Education

In School

From the day you start school, your parents probably try to give you the best education they can. They know that the better educated you are, the more likely you are to get a well paid job and lead a more fulfilling life.

Kindergarten education is important.

Literacy

Literacy means being able to read and write. Every country of the world tries to educate their population so that each individual can develop their knowledge and achieve their goals in life. High literacy rates are enjoyed in all industrial countries, although only Norway, of the larger countries, can boast a 100% literacy level. Poor literacy holds countries back – in Afghanistan, for example, 43% of the men are literate but only 12.6% of the women. This limits how mothers can help and encourage their children with learning.

Many children will spend 10 to 12 years in school.

University students receive their degree certificates when they finish their studies.

High-low earners

The more you can earn, the better off your country becomes. A country that produces lots of high earners such as engineers, computer programmers, doctors and so on, is almost certainly going to have a high GDP. A country in which most people have just a primary school education or where wealth may be based on family farming, will probably have a lower GDP.

Influences: Population

The total number of people living in a country is known as its population. In most countries, the birth of each child and the death of each family member must be recorded with the authorities. So the population figure is generally accurate.

Up and Down

The world population is the total number of living humans on Earth. Today, it is estimated to be over 7.1 billion people. The numbers have grown steadily since the 1300s, with the fastest growth during the 1950 to 1960s. But since 1963, the rate of growth has slowed. However, there is still a worry that the planet will not have enough water, food and energy resources for all.

Over a billion...

China was worried that its population was growing too fast. So, in 1979, it passed a law forbidding couples to have more than one child. There were exceptions for about a third of the population, but most people had to obey the law or face a heavy fine. Today, the law is relaxed to allow two children for many more people. And China's birth rate is falling anyway, as more women take control of their lives.

Young World

Just over a quarter of the world's population is aged under 15. In another 10 years, these will be the workforce. But will there be too many people on the planet by then - or not enough?

The size of families is declining worldwide due to higher living standards and better work opportunities for women. In Japan, for example, this is seen as a real problem. For the 3rd year running, Japan has reported a low birth rate which does not replace the population that is dying. There are now far more old people than young ones. Soon there will be fewer workers and fewer consumers to keep the economy going.

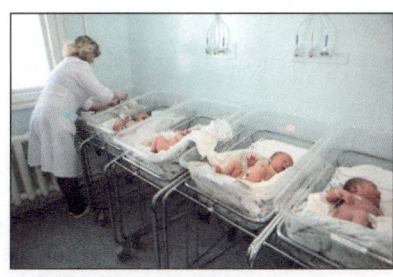

Newborn babies in the hospital ward.

A large, young population is a healthy sign for a country's economy.

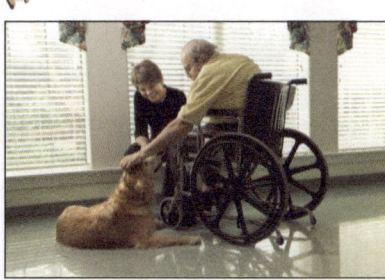

The cost of caring for the elderly comes from the tax contribution of the younger workforce.

Most Populated Countries
(people in billions and millions)

- 1 China   1,364,600,000
- 2 India   1,244,430,000
- 3 United States   318,087,000
- 4 Indonesia   247,424,598
- 5 Brazil   202,598,000
- 6 Pakistan   186,527,000
- 7 Nigeria   173,615,000
- 8 Bangladesh   152,518,015
- 9 Russia   143,700,000
- 10 Japan   127,100,000

Influences: Labour

In many countries, the economy works because of its **workforce**. This term describes the people who live and work there, their skills and the jobs they do to earn money.

The Workforce

In many countries, people work from the time they leave school or college, or some form of training, until they reach retirement age. They will have worked for 40 years or more, and they stop at that point to enjoy their later age.

Once educated and trained, workers give their skills to many different kinds of jobs. If businesses are succeeding, even growing, more people will be employed. Their earnings are used to buy things, and this keeps money moving through shops, offices and factories, and the whole economy is active.

Training

Almost every job needs some form of training after education ends. It may take years before a person is fully trained and can contribute.

Work Ethic

Some countries are known for the hard work their workers do. People are willing to work hard both for themselves and for the good of their country. We say they have a strong **work ethic**. Countries with this kind of attitude among the workforce tend to have the fastest growing economies.

Labour Market

A country may have a large workforce – lots of people able to work for a living – but they may not have the right skills or live close to where the jobs are, or not be willing to do the jobs available.

The term 'labour market' describes how employees – willing workers – and employers – the people who wish to employ them – come together to produce something. They agree what the job is, where and how long the work will be done, and how much pay or other reward there will be.

Cities attract a large workforce and the labour market operates freely.

Some jobs require the skills of a whole team.

Cheaper-Faster

Some countries are short of people to perform certain skills and jobs. Perhaps these jobs are repetitive and boring. Maybe the wages aren't very high. So employers need to import labour from another country to help out. Or they employ the same people abroad and import the finished goods.

Young people often work long hours at repetitive jobs and for little money.

Child Labour

It's a sad fact that some countries have many young people with little or no education. Here, company bosses employ them to do unskilled and often dangerous work, with long hours and little pay. This is known as child labour, and it is a world problem. Over 150 million children throughout the world aged between 5 and 14 are working and not in school.

Influences: Technology; Industry; Services

Influences: Technology

It's easy to forget that using the computer as a daily tool is a new thing. Your grandparents watched TV on a solid, boxed screen, at first in black and white. You'd be wild if you were asked to do the same!

Communications

Communications, as we know it, are very recent. Only a few hundred years ago, if you wanted to tell somebody something, you had to write a letter. You could only find out what was going on in the world through talking or reading a newspaper – that's if you could read. But with the development of electricity, everything began to change.

Skilled workers assemble high-tech equipment.

Space technology opens up new communication methods.

Now, in our world of advanced technology, everyone can be in touch with just the click of a button. And this has changed the way people work and the way countries make their money.

Computers can design holographic buildings for architects.

Keeping up

Countries at the forefront of the technology revolution have done well.

That's because there is a worldwide demand for technology such as computers and mobile phones. Some Asian countries lead the world in the production and manufacture of electronic technology. Your phone may have been bought at home but it was probably made in China, Korea or Japan.

Losing out

Countries that don't have a technology base tend to lose out. They have to import gadgets, and that means money moves out of their country and into the country of manufacture. This is also a period of great change in the way we communicate, and this means changing the way we train in skills. Countries that provide high-tech education create a useful workforce for the technology industry. Those that don't may lose out.

CREATIVITY

Every invention that has ever been dreamt up has come from the brain of a truly creative person. Creativity is where new ideas are born.

Today, in a world where there is lots of competition and rivalry between companies, someone who has a fresh approach to problems – a person who can "think outside the box" – is welcome in many innovative companies.

Creativity comes with knowledge. If you understand science, or maths, or geography, or economics – or your chosen subject – really well, you are more likely to be an inventor of the future.

Influences: Industry

Industry usually means the manufacture, or making, of goods. In the 1700s and 1800s, new inventions made it possible to produce goods in large quantities and at lower cost. Factories sprang up, and countries that encouraged these industries became rich.

A conveyer belt carries goods from process to process by machine.

Making goods

Making goods provides work for a country's people. If the products are of high enough quality, the country gains a good reputation from selling both at home and abroad. Manufacturing also helps spread the money around, as factory workers spend their wages on different goods and services.

The basic materials

It's not necessarily easy to set up a manufacturing base. Most products are made from some kind of raw material. It's best if the raw materials come from the same country. If they have to be imported from another country, the costs will go up as well as the price of the finished product.

Specialists

With the right raw materials and the right kinds of workers, countries can become specialists at producing certain goods.

In the United States, the automobile industry became one specialist sector. Companies, such as Ford and General Motors, produced cars for the American market as well as for export abroad. Now, both Japan and Korea have created a successful position in the automobile market. People all over the globe drive their cars.

In the United Kingdom, the major players no longer manufacture. But small specialist carmakers have taken over, producing sports cars and other small volume vehicles.

TOURISM

Countries that have lots of beautiful countryside or old cities and towns, historic sites or some special or curious landmark, may get visited by people from other countries. People are always eager to travel to new places and see how others live.

Visitors from abroad, called tourists, need hotels. They need food and transport. They pay to visit places and for entertainment. They spend their money in YOUR country. This is called the tourism industry, and in many countries it is a big, big earner!

Influences: Services

As well as making things to sell, an economy also needs businesses that supply people with things such as banking, insurance, medical or legal services. Service industries like these provide products that you can't easily see, but, just like manufactured goods, they can earn lots of money for a country.

Developed countries

Service industries are usually found in more developed countries such as the USA, Great Britain and other European countries, and Asian countries such as Singapore and Korea. These all have a strong economy, good education and a well-educated workforce.

A growing sector

The service sector has grown steadily over the last hundred years. In the United States, for instance, it earned half the country's GDP in 1929. Fifty years later, it was earning two thirds, and by 1993, more than three quarters. Service industries now add up to more than three fifths of the world's total earnings.

Mechanisation

One reason that the service sector has grown so much is that manufacturing goods has become more and more mechanised. Machines, rather than people, now do much of the work. Fewer people are needed and so more importance is placed on the service jobs of distribution, advertising, management and finance.

Office Workers

Governments have grown in size over the years. This means they need to employ more people. And government employees are all people involved in the service sector.

Of course, there are many people who work in offices in many of the service industries.

SERVICE INDUSTRIES

These are the top 20 service industries around the world:

Advertising
Child care companies
Entertainment
Financial services
Health care
Hospitality industry – hotels
Insurance
Lawyers, solicitors
Marketing and selling
Online services
Tourism
Travel

Influences: Agriculture

Farming and growing produce is all part of an important industry called agriculture. At one time, it was the most important industry because it provided food for a country or food surpluses that could be traded for other things. Today, fewer people are involved in agriculture, but it's still as important an industry as it ever was.

Subsistence

Subsistence farming usually means growing things for your own use. A subsistence farm plants or raises only the crops and animals that the family will need. Little or nothing is left over to trade or sell.

However, many subsistence farmers try to trade surplus crops for things they can't grow such as sugar, clothing and iron roofing. Most subsistence farmers live in poor or developing countries in rural Africa and Asia. Some have developed trade contacts and links, selling items that use their specialised skills and local materials.

Surplus

When farmers grow stuff mostly to sell, they sometimes produce more than they can get rid of. This is called a **surplus**. You might think that the best way to get rid of surplus wheat or butter would be to give it to countries with starving populations. But that doesn't work because it would lower the price of the commodity generally and farmers would make little profit.

So what happens to the surplus? Sometimes it builds up and is left to rot. More likely it is 'dumped', which means it's sold off cheaply.

Huge fields like this provide a rich harvest of rape oil.

Surplus wheat is piled high.

Fair Trade

Fair trade is a policy that helps poorer farmers in developing countries. It aims to make sure that those who produce commodities for sale abroad are not exploited or do not lose out through unfair trade and tariffs. The coffee and banana sectors are current examples.

Unfortunately, rich countries still make it difficult for poor farmers to compete. They demand proof that all produce will be of a high quality which isn't always possible.

Subsidies

From time to time, governments help out farmers by giving **subsidies**. A subsidy is some form of financial help. It may be in the form of a direct payment of money, a tax reduction or a cheaper rate for things such as water.

Goods are transported using manpower.

A small catch must earn enough to feed the family.

Traditional farming methods in use.

Surplus foods are sold at market.

Import - Export

Most countries tend to concentrate on producing goods and services which they can make better or cheaper than other countries. If they make more than they need themselves, they can then trade the surplus with other nations.

Exports

Exports are goods and services that are supplied to and bought by companies or governments in other countries. Exporting, or selling lots of goods abroad, is good for a country because it brings cash in and creates wealth.

Imports

Goods and services that are brought into a country to sell are called imports. Imports cost nations money because the company that imports them has to pay for them. So, money moves out of the country.

TOP EXPORTER
China exports more than any other country.

TOP IMPORTER
The USA imports more than any other country.

KEEPING A BALANCE
A country's trade balance is about what the country has sold abroad and what it has bought from abroad.

The difference between what a country sells and what it buys is the trade gap.

However, most countries don't want a big gap between what they buy and what they sell. They try to find a balance, known as a trade balance, between their exports and their imports. So when they export a great deal, they also tend to import a great deal as well.

Stop-start!

Many people think that governments should not interfere too much in the economy of a country. They believe that business people know what they are doing and know how to make money.

Free to trade

Those who support working in a free market say that when a government interferes too much, businesses don't work well. Business owners should be able to decide themselves how much to pay their workers and how much they can export – in fact, how to run their own businesses.

They say business owners will lose interest in growing their business if they can't make the maximum profit.

Controls on trade

Other people believe that governments should be involved in business and that they can help.

In this way, governments make rules that businesses have to stand by. Among other things, they can introduce rules to help their own country's trade and to stop other countries from taking this business. They do this by interfering in the free market. They create barriers to hinder competition. These are known as trade barriers.

BARRIERS

A trade barrier is anything that hinders trade.

Tariffs are special taxes on imported goods that make them more expensive. The purpose of the tariff is to make domestic goods cheaper than the imported ones.

Quotas limit the amount of imported goods that can enter a country within a certain period of time. Of course, domestic companies have no such limits.

Product standards can also be used as a barrier to trade. For example, some countries do not permit the import of genetically altered (GM) beef or wheat. This protects local farmers from competition too.

A stable government

In some countries, the government changes often. In others, the government remains in place for a fixed term, say four years.

If the government is involved in how businesses run and create wealth for the country, it doesn't help if they keep changing. Changing governments might introduce new rules and regulations just when a business is getting used to the old ones. So, stable governments – ones that stay around for a fixed period – are better for business.

A part to play

Wherever you live, you'll be expected to contribute to your country's economy once you are an adult. Whether you work as a lawyer, a nurse, a cab driver – or whatever, you're going to be part of what makes your country wealthy.

Getting educated

It starts with your education. Most developed countries offer free education at least until high school level. Governments control the education system to make sure young people have the basic skills to make their way in life, such as the ability to read or do basic mathematics and computer operations.

Higher education prepares students in more specialised ways. A university degree may prepare you for a professional career while a technical college might prepare you to enter an industry.

Choosing a career

You may be good at something from an early age that points you in the direction of a particular career. If you're really good at maths, for instance, you might want to train as a teacher or take a degree in physics that leads you to astronomy. If you're not sure which career you want to choose, there are career instructors in schools to help you.

Getting trained

Your education may not end with school. Training in specialist skills is often carried out in the workplace. Companies may offer apprenticeships where you can learn a trade while you work. Other agencies also offer training courses to help with basic skills.

Location

There are places in many countries where specific jobs are carried out. The technology sector is big in an area of California, USA, called 'Silicon Valley', for instance. The financial sector thrives in one area of London called 'The City'. If you want to do the job you're trained for, you may have to move to where the job exists.

Today, populations are more mobile, and people are more willing to go to the right place for them. Mobility helps the economy, although some people would argue that one area's success means another area's failure and that work opportunities should be more evenly spread.

Your Contribution

Once you're working, you're contributing to the economy. You do this through the taxes you pay and the money you spend. Whether you're buying a new car, a house or food to eat, you're putting money into the economy that allows other people to thrive and contribute as well.

And it doesn't matter what you do, or how much you earn – once you are working you are helping the economy to grow and your country to prosper.

Let's discuss

Is taxation fair?

All countries have to raise money, so most apply taxes to their working population. Different countries ask for different amounts. And usually, the more you earn, the more you have to pay. Is it fair to tax the rich more heavily than low paid workers? Or should everyone pay the same amount regardless of how much they earn?

Printing money

Does printing money solve financial problems? Countries are responsible for printing their money. They can print as much as they want to. So if a country gets into financial trouble, why not just print more notes?

Is inflation a bad thing?

Inflation means rising prices. Some economists argue that a small amount of inflation is not a bad thing. Others say that inflation has to be kept low or removed altogether. Why is inflation considered to be bad for an economy?

Is child labour justified?

In some countries, children are allowed to work long hours for low pay. This may help keep costs down, make products competitive and boost the economy. But can child labour anywhere be considered acceptable?

What's your currency like?

Could you come up with a better design? Whose head would you have on YOUR currency? What colours and what pattern?

What job will you do in the future?

The world is constantly changing – and now quicker than ever. Jobs that existed fifty years ago may not exist now. How can education help you choose the right job for the future and how do you know that it will exist in just a few years time? Is easy access to retraining the answer?

What does your country export?

Exporting goods or services can help a country's economy grow. Countries that can produce goods more cheaply than others will do well. But that might mean low wages and poor working conditions. Is that the right way to go? What goods or services does your country export?

Glossary

birth rate
The rate at which a country can measure and compare the number of babies born in a given period of time.

brand
A mark or name on a manufacturer's products which is easily recognised.

budget deficit
The difference between what a country needs to pay for all its obligations and the money it has available to do so.

commodity
The name given to essential products such as grains and metals that are bought and sold in large quantities.

communications
A general term that describes ways in which people pass information to each other using modern technology.

consumer spending
A description of how people spend their money and how much they spend.

debt
Borrowed money to be repaid.

democracy
A system of running a country in which the people who live there choose their government.

economy
The financial and business activity of a country.

export
To sell goods and services abroad to earn money for the country.

fossil fuel
Fuels such as coal and petrol that are found in the earth where they have developed over millions of years.

free market
A way an economy can work where businesses are free to operate as they please with no government rules.

government
The group of people elected to run a country on behalf of its people.

Gross Domestic Product
The total earnings of a country. This is often referred to as GDP.

health care
A government-run programme that makes sure all people receive some form of medical care.

import
To buy goods and services from a foreign country.

income
Another name for earnings.

income tax
A tax paid to the government by people who earn a certain amount.

inflation
The way in which money loses value as the cost of goods and services rises and it is able to purchase less.

investment
Money lent to a person or company to help it trade.

labour market
The total number of people available to work in a country, or using a particular skill.

literacy
The ability to read and write to a basic level.

natural resource
Something that is naturally available in an environment, such as water or oil or forests. A workforce is also a natural resource.

poverty
The state of not having enough money for basic needs.

quota
A restriction set by a government on how much of something can be imported or exported.

raw material
A material such as timber or metal which can be turned into some other product.

recession
The state of an economy when it starts to slow down and not earn enough.

services
Activities such as schools and museums paid for by local governments.

subsidy
A government payment made to help a business or service.

surplus
Extra goods that are not used locally and which may not be needed abroad either.

tariff
A tax set by the government of a country to make imports more expensive.

tax
A part of income or payments, collected by governments for general use.

tax haven
A country that sets very low, or even no, tax levels.

wage
Money earned on a regular basis in exchange for work.

work ethic
The desire to work hard for a living.

workforce
The people who work in a country or a business.

Index

The Great Depression 25
agriculture 3, 6, 9, 15, 32, 35, 50
bank 17, 21
banknotes 8
bankrupt 15
birth rate 40, 41
blank 17
border 5, 7, 30, 31, 34
budget deficit 24
business 12, 13, 15, 20, 21, 23, 27, 28, 34, 36, 42, 48, 54, 55
cars 11, 13, 37, 47
China 40, 53
climate 2, 28, 32
commodity 22, 37, 50
communications 44
conflict 38
consumer 41
consumer spending 20, 21
corruption 29
creativity 45
crop 33
currency 2, 16, 17, 18, 19, 38, 59
debt 7, 24, 35, 60
defence 7
democracy 27
Denmark 13
distribution 21, 49
dollar 16
drought 33
economist 21
economy 3, 15, 22, 24, 29, 38, 42
education 3, 6, 9, 29, 39
electronics 45
employment 6, 9, 24, 43, 49
energy 21, 35, 36, 37, 40
expenditure 8, 9
export 35, 47, 51, 52, 53, 54, 59
factory 5, 20, 23, 42
Fair Trade 51
finance minister 27
food 4, 11, 33, 36, 40, 47, 50, 57
fossil fuel 36
free market 54
geography 30
goods 52
government 5, 7, 9, 10, 11, 12, 13, 14, 15, 21, 23, 25, 26, 27, 49, 54, 55, 60
grant 6
Greece 35
greenhouse effect 33
Gross Domestic Product (GDP) 2, 22, 23, 35, 39, 48
health care 13, 60
housing 7, 9
import 3, 13, 43, 45, 53, 55
Incas 11
income 8, 12, 13, 21, 24, 60

income tax 11
industry 3, 6, 24, 46, 48
inflation 23
intaglio 17
interest 7, 9, 14, 21, 54
investment 23, 24, 25, 60
job 13, 15, 21, 25, 27, 39, 42, 43, 49, 57
labour market 43
literacy 39
loan 7
lottery 14
machinery 34, 51
manufacture 17, 45, 46, 47, 48, 49
mechanisation 49
minting 17
money 52
national health scheme 7
natural resource 21, 28, 34, 35, 36
Norway 35, 39

oil 36
physical barriers 28
plastic 36
politics 29
population 15, 30, 35, 39, 40, 41
power 26, 27, 34, 35
product 20, 21, 22, 29, 46, 48, 60
profit 23, 50, 54
quota 55
raw material 22, 46, 47
recession 24
republic 26
savings bonds 14
school 5, 26, 39, 42, 43, 56, 57, 60
services 3, 9, 11, 20, 21, 22, 46, 48, 52, 60
shareholder 23
slump 24
social protection 6, 9
subsidy 6, 23, 51

subsistence farming 50
surplus 50, 51
tariff 38, 51
tax 2, 6, 7, 10, 11, 12, 13, 21, 23, 27, 41, 51, 55, 57, 60
tax haven 13
tax threshold 12
technology 3, 44
tourism 47
trade 21, 22, 24, 28, 29, 30, 31, 34, 35, 38, 50, 51, 52, 53, 54, 55, 57, 60
trade balance 53
trade gap 53
training 42, 57
transport 7, 9
unemployment 6, 25
war 38
wealth 22, 52
work ethic 29, 42
workforce 3, 12, 41, 42, 43, 45, 48

63

绿色印刷　保护环境　爱护健康

亲爱的读者朋友：

本书已入选"北京市绿色印刷工程——优秀出版物绿色印刷示范项目"。它采用绿色印刷标准印制，在封底印有"绿色印刷产品"标志。

按照国家环境标准（HJ2503—2011）《环境标志产品技术要求 印刷 第一部分：平版印刷》，本书选用环保型纸张、油墨、胶水等原辅材料，生产过程注重节能减排，印刷产品符合人体健康要求。

选择绿色印刷图书，畅享环保健康阅读！

北京市绿色印刷工程

图书在版编目（CIP）数据

国家货币：国家是如何花钱的？为什么要花钱？：汉、英／（英）怀特海德，（英）劳，（英）贝利著；（英）比奇插图；傅瑞蓉译. —北京：华夏出版社，2016.1

（华夏少儿金融智慧屋. 货币系列）

书名原文：Country Money: How Countries Spend Their Money, and Why?

ISBN 978-7-5080-8702-3

Ⅰ.①国… Ⅱ.①怀… ②劳… ③贝… ④比… ⑤傅… Ⅲ.①国家财政—少儿读物—汉、英 Ⅳ.①F81-49

中国版本图书馆CIP数据核字（2015）第306746号

Country Money: How Countries Spend Their Money, and Why?
Copyright © 2014 BrambleKids Ltd
All rights reserved
The simplified Chinese translation rights arranged through Rightol Media（本书中文简体版权经由锐拓传媒取得 Email:copyright@rightol.com）
CHINESE SIMPLIFIED Language adaptation edition published by BrambleKids Ltd., and HUAXIA PUBLISHING HOUSE Copyright © 2016
All Rights Reserved

版权所有　翻版必究
北京市版权局著作权合同登记号：图字 01-2015-2440

国家货币——国家是如何花钱的？为什么要花钱？

作　者	［英］威廉·怀特海德　［英］费利西娅·劳　［英］格里·贝利
插　图	［英］马克·比奇
译　者	傅瑞蓉
责任编辑	李雪飞
出版发行	华夏出版社
经　销	新华书店
印　装	北京中科印刷有限公司
版　次	2016年1月北京第1版　　2016年1月北京第1次印刷
开　本	787×1030　1/16
印　张	8
字　数	140千字
定　价	39.80元

华夏出版社　地址：北京市东直门外香河园北里4号　邮编：100028
网址：www.hxph.com.cn　电话：（010）64663331（转）
若发现本版图书有印装质量问题，请与我社营销中心联系调换。